Roald Martinussen

Overview of

International CISG Sales Law

Basic Contract Law according to the UN Convention on Contracts for the International Sale of Goods (CISG)

© Roald Martinussen 2006

ISBN 1-4196-4448-3

Short overview

Contents in details   5

Chapter 1. The convention's sphere of application   13

Chapter 2. CISG and the contract of sale. Formation   18
2.1 The CISG and the contract. Freedom of contract.   18
2.2 The contract of sale   19

Chapter 3. Delivery, risk and payment   23

3.0 Introduction   23
3.1 Delivery and passing of the risk   23
3.2 The obligation to pay the price   32
3.3 Payment and delivery.   35

Chapter 4. Delivery of the goods   37

4.0 Breach of contract concerning delivery of the goods 37
4.1 Remedies for breach of the contract obligation to deliver the goods   40
4.10 The buyer requires performance.   40
4.11 The buyer declares the contract avoided.   41
4.12 The buyer claims damages.   45

Chapter 5. Conformity of the goods
Breach of Contract by lack of conformity   56

5.0 What is lack of conformity according to the CISG? Introduction.   56
5.1 Remedies for breach of contract by lack of conformity   71
5.2 Third party claims   89

Chapter 6. Obligations of the buyer 93

6.1 Introduction. Delayed or no payment. The buyer's obligation to take delivery. 93
6.2 Remedies for breach of contract by the buyer. 93
6.3 The buyer's obligation to take delivery. 97

Chapter 7. Common provisions 99

7.0 Introduction 99
7.1 Damages 99
7.2 Notification of breach of contract 103
7.3 Return of the goods when the contract is avoided or substitute goods are delivered 109
7.4 Anticipatory breach 112
7.5 Instalment contracts. Breach of a part. 115
7.6 Preservation of the goods 117

CISG index 121

Literature 125

Appendix: United Nations Convention on Contracts for the International Sale of Goods (1980) 126

Contents in details

Preface   11

Chapter 1. The convention's sphere of application   13

1.1 The term «sale of goods»   *13*
1.11 Not goods bought for personal, family and household use.   *14*
1.12 Manufactured or produced goods.   *14*
1.13 Sales and services. Combined contracts   *15*

Chapter 2. CISG and the contract of sale. Formation

2.1 The CISG and the contract. Freedom of contract.   18

2.10 Introduction.   *18*
2.11 Usage   *18*

2.2 The contract of sale   19

2.21 Formation of the contract.   *19*
2.22 Interpretation of the contract of sale.   *21*

Chapter 3. Delivery, risk and payment   23

3.0 Introduction   23

3.1 Delivery and passing of the risk   23

3.10 Introduction.   *23*
3.11 What is «risk»?   *24*
3.12 The principal rule concerning passing of the risk.   *26*
3.13 The passing of risk and place of delivery.   *26*

3.14 Exception: Extended risk for the buyer.	*28*
3.15 Exception: Extended risk for the seller.	*29*
3.16 Goods sold in transit.	*30*
3.17 Time of delivery, article 33 and 34	*31*

3.2 The obligation to pay the price   32

3.20 What price to pay.	*32*
3.21 Place and time of payment.	*34*

3.3 Payment and delivery.   35

Chapter 4. Delivery of the goods   37

4.0 Breach of contract concerning delivery of the goods   37

4.00 Introduction.   *37*

4.1 Remedies for breach of the contract obligation to deliver the goods   40

4.10 The buyer requires performance.	*40*
4.100 Introduction.	*40*
4.11 The buyer declares the contract avoided.	*41*
4.110 Introduction.	*41*
4.111 Fundamental breach.	*41*
4.112 Additional period of time. Notification.	*43*
4.12 The buyer claims damages.	*45*
4.120 Introduction.	*45*
4.121 Damages for breach of contract for delayed or no delivery.	*46*
4.122 Delayed delivery due to a third person.	*52*
4.123 Liability for temporary impediments.	*54*
4.124 Notification of impediment.	*54*

Chapter 5. Conformity of the goods
Breach of Contract by lack of conformity 56

5.0 What is lack of conformity according to the CISG? 56

5.00 *Introduction.* 56
5.01 *To read the contract is the first step* . 56
5.02 *The purpose of the contract.* 57
5.03 *Price and quality.* 61
5.04 *Time for judgment on conformity.* 62
5.05 *Longevity of the goods.* 64
5.06 *The goods' accordance with a sample or model.* 66
5.07 *The buyer's examination of the goods. Negligence.* 67

5.1 Remedies for breach of contract by lack of conformity 71

5.10 *Introduction.* 71
5.11 *Remedy of the lack of conformity (by repair or by substitute goods).* 72
5.110 *Introduction.* 72
5.111 *The buyer requires performance according to the contract.* 73
5.112 *The seller's right to remedy lack of conformity.* 76
5.113 *The buyer's obligation to accept the seller's remedying of the lack of conformity.* 79
5.12 *Price reduction.* 79
5.13 *The buyer declares the contract avoided.* 82
5.130 *Introduction* 82
5.131 *Fundamental breach.* 83
5.132 *Notification.* 84
5.14 *The buyer claims damages.* 86
5.141 *Lack of conformity due to a third person.* 89

5.2 Third party claims 89

Chapter 6. Obligations of the buyer 93

6.1 Introduction. Delayed or no payment. The buyer's obligation to take delivery. 93

6.2 Remedies for breach of contract by the buyer. 94

6.20 The seller requires the buyer to perform his obligations.
94
6.200 Introduction. *94*
6.201 Interest *94*
6.21 The seller declares the contract avoided *95*
6.210 Fundamental breach. *95*
6.211 Additional period of time. *96*
6.22 The seller claims damages. *96*

6.3 The buyer's obligation to take delivery. 97

Chapter 7 Common provisions 99

7.0 Introduction 99

7.1 Damages 99

7.10 Principal conditions for claiming damages *99*
7.11 Price difference. *100*
7.12 A party's obligation to mitigate his losses. *102*

7.2 Notification of breach of contract 103

7.20 Introduction. *103*
7.21 Notification directly following the breach of contract.
104
7.22 Notification within two years. *108*

7.3 Return of the goods when the contract is avoided or substitute goods are delivered   **109**

7.30 Introduction.   *109*
7.31 Restitution substantially in the condition in which he received the goods, CISG chapter V.   *110*

7.4 Anticipatory breach.   **112**

7.5 Instalment contracts. Breach of a part.   **115**

7.6 Preservation of the goods   **117**

CISG index   **121**

Literature   **125**

<u>Appendix:</u> United Nations Convention on Contracts for the International Sale of Goods (1980)   **126**

Preface

CISG Introduction

The Convention on Contracts for the International Sale of Goods was completed in Vienna 1980-04-11. The number of members of the convention is now approaching 100 countries from all over the world and of all political and cultural systems.

In the legal system the sales law is part of the contract law, which again is part of the law of the obligations and the private law.

The full text of the CISG is included in an appendix in this book, and should be used when reading the book.

The CISG index will help to find comments on a specific article in the convention.

This book aims to give both students and practitioners who are working with contracts, an introduction to contract law and to the CISG. Therefore this book is rather short and can only serve as an overview of the main articles of the CISG and thereby of the legal system of contract law. For further studies and more extensive comments on specific articles and when contract problems occur, a wide range of more voluminous books on the CISG have been published.

CISG cases, which can be found on the Internet, may deepen the insight while working with the CISG.

Stavanger, Norway, summer 2006

Roald Martinussen

Chapter 1: The convention's sphere of application

1.1 The term «sale of goods».

The CISG's sphere of application is found in article 1, which says that the convention applies to «sale of goods» (art 1 (1). The convention does not say much to explain this specific term, even though article 3, as we shall see, decides on the application of the term under certain circumstances. Article 2, however, expresses certain types of sales to which the convention *does not* apply:

«This Convention does not apply to sales:
(a) of goods bought for personal, family or household use, unless the seller, at any time before or at the conclusion of the contract, neither knew nor ought to have known that the goods were bought for any such use;
(b) by auction;
(c) on execution or otherwise by authority of law;
(d) of stocks, shares, investment securities, negotiable instruments or money;
(e) of ships, vessels, hovercraft or aircraft;
(f) of electricity.»

The convention thus applies to the undertaking of a certain type of contracts, namely contract for the international sale of goods. Other types of contracts are then excluded. Since the term international suggests that the goods are to be transported from one country to another, sales of real estate are, by a reasonable interpretation of the term, excluded. And the convention itself excludes goods like ships, vessels, hovercraft or aircraft, which are goods of extraordinary size and legal complexity.

What is sale of goods, then? The contract typically gives the parties *mutual rights and obligations.* Furthermore one of the contracting parties will have the obligation of paying money.

The main intention of the contract of sale is for the buyer to come in both legal and practical possession of the goods. He is the new owner. Thus the seller accordingly loses these rights.

The question of who owns the goods may occur in several ways: The buyer wishes to use the goods or he wants to sell them to a new buyer. The creditor, whom the buyer owes money, and/or the seller, may try to take possession of the goods for their legal claims. Conflicts may then occur concerning who owns the goods. Such questions are handled in other parts of the legal system, not exclusively in the law of contract.

We can define goods as objects that are sold. By goods we naturally refer to physical, concrete products, which we can feel and see. This is also the way the convention sees it. See article 2, letter d), which excludes goods like «stocks, shares, investment securities, negotiable instruments, and electricity».

1.11 The convention does not apply to products bought for personal, family and household use.

According to article 2, letter a), CISG *does not* apply to sales «of goods bought for personal, family or household use». If a consumer buys goods for consumer use, the CISG does not apply. The convention *does apply*, however, to sale of consumer products, like consumer electronics and cars, if the goods are meant to be sold by the buyer in his business.

1.12 Manufactured or produced goods.

CISG applies to the contract even if the goods, which will eventually be delivered, do not exist at the time of contract formation, but are to be manufactured by the seller, article 3 (1). This is called manufactured or produced goods. CISG does not apply, however, if «the party who orders the goods undertakes to supply a substantial part of the materials necessary for such manufacture or production».

A contract, for example, in which a bakery is to bake a cake according to given specifications, will then be a sale according to CISG. But if the buyer sends animal skins to a tailor asking him to manufacture a fur jacket from it, the CISG will not apply to the contract.

1.13 Sales and services. Combined contracts.

Contracts for pure services are not sales according to CISG. It is quite obvious that a labour contract is not a sales contract, and this is also the case with other contracts for performance of services. CISG does not apply. CISG article 3 (2) draws a line between sales and services. The decisive point is whether «the preponderant part of the obligations of the party who furnishes the goods consists in the supply of labour or other services».

But it is also important to be able to draw a line between article 3 paragraphs (1) and (2). If the contract in question is a contract for the supply of goods to be manufactured or produced, we can *not* take article 3 (2) into consideration and thus ask whether the manufacturers amount of labour is *preponderant* or not. What matters in article 3 (1) is which party shall supply «*a substantial part of the materials necessary*» for the manufacture or production.

A guiding point of view when drawing the line between article 3 (1) and 3 (2) may be to observe *when* the labour is to take place: If the labour is to take place *before* delivery, it is a contract for the supply of goods to be manufactured or produced and we shall use article 3 (1).

However, if the labour or the services are to take place *during or after* delivery we have to use article 3 (2).

For example: The buyer orders a painting from a famous painter and is willing to pay accordingly. The painter will supply materials needed to fulfil the order. Delivery can obviously not take place before the painting is finished. According to article 3 (1), this contract is one for the supply of goods to be manufactured or produced, and CISG will apply since the buyer is not supplying materials. CISG will apply even if the materials are of little value compared to the value of the famous painter's work.

Another reason why article 3 (2) does not apply to this contract is that this paragraph mentions goods and labour as two separate obligations. This fact suggests that the labour or services come as an appendix to the obligation to supply goods. In article 3 (2) the labour or services do not consist of producing or manufacturing the goods, as is the case in article 3 (1).

When we in article 3 (2) draw the line between sales and services, it is decisive, as seen above, whether or not the services or labour represent the preponderant part of the seller's obligations. If this is the case, the whole contract falls outside of CISG's sphere of application, including the part that consists of the supply of goods. And then the other way around: If the preponderant part of the contract is the supply of goods, CISG applies to the contract as a whole, and not only to the labour or service part of it. When we decide which part of the contract is «the preponderant part», it is fair to start with an economic evaluation. Preponderant means more than half the value of the contract. If the labour or services are stipulated to more than half the sum that the buyer has to pay, article 3 (2) itself clearly decides that CISG does not apply.

If this is not the case, it is correct to interpret article 3 (2) antithetic so that CISG *does apply* to the contract. The sum of money is not the only way to evaluate, however. In some cases it may be reasonable to look at the whole contract as a contract for supply of labour and services:

This may be the case with an engine repair contract including change of parts in the engine. The purpose of this contract is to achieve a well functioning engine, and it is the professional task of the contract party who has undertaken to do just that, to examine the case and see to it that the engine functions well after the repair. If he ends up with changing an expensive part, which value exceeds the value of this contract party's professional labour, we may still find it reasonable to call the contract a repair contract and not a contract for sale and installing of an engine particle. Consequently CISG will not apply to this repair contract.

However, with contracts for sale of new goods to be installed, and the installation itself is relatively simple and does not call upon greater expertise, the CISG *does apply* to the contract.

As we have now seen, whether or not the sale or the services are preponderant according to article 3 (2) is not always easy to decide. In each individual case we will have to consider all relevant information.

Chapter 2 CISG and the contract of sale. Formation

2.1 The CISG and the contract. Freedom of contract.

2.10 Introduction.

According to CISG article 6 the convention has a status as background law, which is only applicable as far as the contract parties themselves have not decided on the matter in their contract. Many contracts, especially uncomplicated sales, only stipulate type and quantity of the goods, the price and, may be, some quality requirements, and then the rest is thereby left to the CISG to decide on. Sales contracts of greater size and complexity, however, are likely to go into more details about the goods and their delivery and payment. Such contracts will to a greater extent avoid the CISG. In some cases the contract is complete to the extent that hardly any articles of the CISG will be applicable.

2.11 Usage.

Article 9 states that «the parties are bound by any usage to which they have agreed and by any practices which they have established between themselves». When the parties are tied to matters on which they have agreed, they are already following the above mentioned article 6, and the parties' agreement replaces the CISG on such matters. Article 9 states that the parties are tied to any practices which they have established between themselves, even if a practice may not have been specifically agreed on in the present contract. Such practices bind the parties and replace the correspondent articles in the CISG.

Article 9 (2) goes on to consider the parties impliedly bound by other usages, which are widely known in international trade. This is so if the parties know or ought to have known about that particular usage. If the parties do not want such usages to apply, they have to state otherwise in their contract.

2.2 The contract of sale

2.21 Formation of the contract.

A contract is concluded when one party makes a proposal and the other party then accepts this proposal, see article 23. According to article 14, a proposal has to be «sufficiently definite» and also indicate the intention of the party who makes the proposal (called «offeror» in the convention) to be bound in case of acceptance. What makes a proposal «sufficiently definite»? Article 14 (1) 2nd sentence answers: «A proposal is sufficiently definite if it indicates the goods and expressly or implicitly fixes or makes provision for determining the quantity and the price. »

According to article 18 (2) an acceptance of an offer becomes effective «at the moment the indication of assent reaches the offeror».

If the other contract party's accept does not match the proposal, even if it has the form of an acceptance, article 19 (1) applies: «A reply to an offer which purports to be an acceptance but contains additions, limitations or other modifications is a rejection of the offer and constitutes a counter-offer.»

This counter-offer is then subject to consideration by the first offeror, who may accept, decline or send a counter-offer. This may continue until we eventually have an offer and an acceptance that match each other. The process may be more complex if the parties meet at a conference table and negotiate a deal because in such a process it may be difficult to pinpoint the exact moment they have reached a binding agreement. Therefore many parties agree on how the process is to take place before they start negotiating, for instance agree that no binding contract exists before both parties has signed a draft or a contract.

An offer (or counter-offer) sent from one of the parties in the process of contract formation becomes effective when it reaches the other party, see article 15 (1). The word «reach» suggests that it is not necessary for him to have read the offer. It is sufficient that the offer has reached the other party, making it up to him whether or not the offer is actually read and when, see article 24. As a consequence an offer (counter-offer) may be withdrawn up until the point when it has reached the other party. Article 15 (2) states that an offer «may be withdrawn if the withdrawal reaches the offeree before or at the same time as the offer». According to articles 22 and 18 (2) this is also the case for an acceptance.

So if a contract party wants to withdraw his offer, counter-offer or acceptance, he has to act quickly in order not to risk getting into legal quick sand. Even *after* this crucial moment there is still a possibility to *revoke* an offer (counter-offer). According to article 16:

«(1) Until a contract is concluded an offer may be revoked if the revocation reaches the offeree before he has dispatched an acceptance.
(2) However, an offer cannot be revoked:
(a) if it indicates, whether by stating a fixed time for acceptance or otherwise, that it is irrevocable; or
(b) if it was reasonable for the offeree to rely on the offer as being irrevocable and the offeree has acted in reliance on the offer.»

Article 16 is a complicated article where a contract party may find himself in need of a lawyer to explain the distinction between withdrawal and revocation. International conferences often turn to complex articles, like article 16, when they have to make a compromise acceptable for legal systems from all over the world. Mostly because of article 16, four contracting countries (Denmark, Finland, Norway and Sweden) used their option according to article 92 (1) to declare that they will not be bound by CISG part II.

An acceptance of an offer has to reach the offeror within the period of time fixed in the offer itself. If no time is fixed by the offeror, article 18 (2) requires acceptance «within a reasonable time, due account being taken of the circumstances of the transaction, including the rapidity of the means of communication employed by the offeror. An oral offer must be accepted immediately unless the circumstances indicate otherwise».

2.22 Interpretation of the contract of sale.

When interpreting the contract we should first of all read the words in their natural meaning according to normal usage of language. Specific technical terms or trade terms are to be used in their usual meaning in that type of business. If the parties have been regular business partners in the past, article 8 (3) prescribes due consideration taken to any such practices established between the parties. This is reasonable because when a practice already exists between the parties, one party should not alone be able to change that practice without an agreement in the contract. We must look at the previous contracts between the parties and see how that particular question has been dealt with in the past.

Article 8 (3) furthermore requires due consideration to the negotiations which took place during the formation of the contract. Any correspondence or notes taken are of interest; if one of the parties has had a suggestion declined at a previous stage, it may be unreasonable to interpret the contract according to that suggestion.

The main goal according to article 8 (3) is to determine «the intent of a party or the understandings a reasonable person would have had». We should thereby consider all available and relevant circumstances of the case. Hereby we must study how the contract or the statement reasonably occurs to the other party, see article 8 (1): «For the purposes of this Convention statements made by and other conduct of a party are to be interpreted according to his intent where the other party knew or could not have been unaware what that intent was.» If the intent cannot be found this way, article 8 (2) applies: «If the preceding paragraph is not applicable, statements made by and other conduct of a party are to be interpreted according to the understanding that a reasonable person of the same kind as the other party would have had in the same circumstances.»

Chapter 3. Delivery, risk and payment

3.0 Introduction

This chapter will look at the practical fulfilment of the contract, while the next chapters concentrate on situations where things do not go according to what has been prescribed in the contract; this is called breach of contract.

We will study the parties' mutual obligations during the fulfilment of the contract; the seller's obligation to deliver the goods and the buyer's obligation to pay for it. We will also try to decide who bears the risk when the goods disappear or are damaged during the process of transportation and delivery.

3.1 Delivery and passing of risk

3.10 Introduction.

The seller's main obligation is to deliver the goods in due time. The seller has to deliver goods as stipulated in the contract, at the right place at the right time. If he does not, we have a breach of contract by the seller, the consequences of which we will approach in the next chapters.

The delivery of the goods is of great importance in other areas as well: When the goods are delivered in accordance with article 31, the risk passes to the buyer in accordance with article 67. Finally the delivery/passing of risk marks the time for deciding on lack of conformity: The seller is only liable for lack of conformity that exists at the time the risk passes to the buyer, article 36 (1).

We see that it is of importance whether the goods are properly delivered or not. Thus it is important which criteria have to be met in order for the goods to be considered delivered. How far must the seller transport the goods in order to fulfil his obligation to deliver them? Up until what point is transportation the responsibility of the seller? And within what time?

3.11 What is «risk»?

A sale aims to transfer the possession of the goods from seller to buyer. A consequence of this fact is that the buyer must obtain the rights to the goods both practically and legally. In most cases this means that the goods must be handed over to the buyer, so called «in natura». But how do we solve questions that arise when something happens to the goods before it is handed over to the buyer, by «loss of or damage to the goods» as article 66 expresses it?

In such situations the urgent question for the parties is whether the buyer is still committed to pay the contract sum (or claim the money back if he has already paid). Article 66 deals with this question when it explains what it means that the risk has passed to the buyer, which is the crucial moment during the transport of the goods from the seller to the buyer.
After this moment «loss of or damage to the goods … does not discharge him [the buyer] from his obligation to pay the price, unless the loss or damage is due to an act or omission of the seller».

Thus «after the risk has passed to the buyer», the buyer is the one who bears the risk and he has to pay the price for the goods even if something should happen to them after the risk has passed.

First of all, this means that the buyer has to pay the price if the goods are damaged because the buyer himself or his employees have not been careful enough, for example when handling or opening the cases. This is fully reasonable. However, it also applies even if the damage is accidental; that is an occasion neither the seller nor the buyer reasonably can take responsibility for. For example lightning hits the goods, the ship carrying the goods goes down, or the train entrails.

If the risk already has passed to the buyer when such an occasion occurs, the buyer will nevertheless have to pay the price. The buyer will then have to raise claims against a third person, for example transporters, who may be responsible for the occasion, or take advantage of the transport insurance, which hopefully has been arranged for in due time.

Article 66, which requires the buyer carrying the risk to pay the price, does not apply when «the loss or damage is due to an act or omission of the seller». If the latter is the case, the buyer may in fact be discharged for his obligation to pay the price even after the risk has passed to him. The loss of the goods or delivery of damaged goods will then represent a breach of contract by the seller according to articles 30 and 35, giving the buyer rights provided in article 45 and the following articles. The parties may for example have agreed that the goods should be sent by a special mail service and marked «careful». Then if the goods are damaged because they are sent by the cheapest ordinary mail service, the damage is obviously «due to an act or omission of the seller».

Above we have examined situations where the goods are damaged *after* the risk has passed to the buyer, since that is what article 66 deals with. If, however, loss of or damage to the goods occurs *before the risk has passed to the buyer*, it is the seller who still bears the risk. According to the contract with the buyer, the seller still has an obligation to «deliver goods which are of the quantity, quality and description required by the contract» (article 35). If the seller, despite what has happened, manages to repair the goods successfully or to supply alternative goods, then there is no breach of contract. But if he *does not* manage, we have a breach of contract of the seller, and the buyer accordingly has his remedies in CISG Section III. When it comes to loss or damage, the seller is now the one who has to raise claims against a third person, for example the transport agency responsible for the accident, or he may benefit from a transport-insurance.

3.12 The principal rule concerning passing of the risk.
The principal rule is article 67 (1): «If the contract of sale involves carriage of the goods and the seller is not bound to hand them over at a particular place, the risk passes to the buyer when the goods are handed over to the first carrier for transmission to the buyer in accordance with the contract of sale.»

If the seller is bound to hand the goods over at a particular place, article 31 gives further instructions: The seller's obligation to deliver consists of «placing the goods at the buyer's disposal at the place where the seller had his place of business at the time of the conclusion of the contract», see article 31 letter c). If the seller and the buyer both «knew that the goods were at, or were to be manufactured or produced at, a particular place», the seller's obligation to deliver consists of «placing the goods at the buyer's disposal at that place», see article 31 letter b).

When the contract of sale involves carriage of the goods, the important term in article 67 (1) is «the first carrier». This means that the risk passes to the buyer when the transmission starts, in the seller's town in the seller's country. The buyer accordingly bears the transport risk from the first carrier and onwards. Local transport, however, within the seller's town/place – from the seller to the first carrier – is the seller's risk. If the first carrier is situated in another town the seller has to bring the goods there to hand it over.

3.13 The passing of risk and place of delivery.

Article 67 (1) leaves it to the parties to agree on the place where the goods are to be handed over: «If the seller is bound to hand the goods over to a carrier at a particular place, the risk does not pass to the buyer until the goods are handed over to the carrier at that place.»

Such agreement may be written down in the contract or it may be agreed upon otherwise, for example by telephone, see article 11. They will often have practices on this «which they have established between themselves», see article 9.

In order to decide on a place to hand over the goods, many contract parties find it useful to choose among transport terms like ex works, fob (free on board), cif (cost, insurance, freight), Delivery at Frontier and a lot of other such terms. The term fob Rotterdam tells us that the place to hand over the goods is Rotterdam, which means that the risk passes to the buyer at the moment the goods are brought on board the ship in Rotterdam for transport by ship to the buyer's port. This is also the case if the term cif is used, but now the seller also has to arrange for transport and insurance, see article 32 (2) and (3). The buyer also bears the risk during transport when the contract uses the term «Ex works» or other similar terms.

However, if «Delivery» terms are used, the risk passes to the buyer when the particular place mentioned is reached, which often is the buyer's hometown. Then *the seller* accordingly bears the transport risk.

The International Chamber of Commerce (ICC) has worked out a great number of transport terms which are regulated in detail in the booklet INCOTERMS. These terms are now widely used in international trade. To choose the most suitable term is important when a contract of sale is negotiated. The negotiations of transport terms will often show which party is most successful in achieving the best contract conditions.

3.14 Exception: Extended risk for the buyer.

Until now we have drawn up the normal situations as to the passing of the risk.

We will now look at some situations where things do not develop as prescribed in the contract.

According to article 69 the risk may pass to the buyer even *before* delivery has taken place. This will be the case if the buyer «commits a breach of contract by failing to take delivery». If the specific contract between this seller and this buyer does not decide otherwise, article 60 will apply:

«The buyer's obligation to take delivery consists:
(a) in doing all the acts which could reasonably be expected of him in order to enable the seller to make delivery; and
(b) in taking over the goods.»

The risk only passes to the buyer, however, if the seller has been ready to deliver (article 67 (1)) and has fulfilled his duties so far. See article 67 (2): «Nevertheless, the risk does not pass to the buyer until the goods are clearly identified to the contract, whether by markings on the goods, by shipping documents, by notice given to the buyer or otherwise.»

The main obligation of the buyer, however, is to pay the price for the goods, see article 53 and 54. If the seller has reason to believe that the buyer will fail to perform his obligations regarding the payment, the seller may, according to article 71 (1), suspend delivery. And if the seller has already dispatched the goods he may, according to article 71 (2), «prevent the handing over of the goods to the buyer».

The articles in the convention concerning the passing of the risk may in certain situations seem unreasonable to a contract party who, despite his best efforts to fulfil the contract, still has to bear the risk. He has tried hard with his full abilities to fulfil the contract, but nevertheless he has to pay for accidents. This is typical for decisions, which have to be made according to the law of contract.

Here it may seem unreasonable that the buyer has to bear the costs of accidents for which he is not to blame. On the other hand it is not reasonable to let the seller bear these costs either.

Of course, it would be en easy decision if we were to choose between the reasonable and the unreasonable. However, the picture is not always black and white, and we often have to choose between two unreasonable alternatives; it is unreasonable to let the buyer pay, but at the same time it is not reasonable to let the seller lose the payment either. These are the cases when the articles on the passing of risk are most important. These articles help us reach a solution in situations where we have to choose between two unappealing alternatives.

3.15 Exception: Extended risk for the seller.

The seller will also in certain situations find himself bearing the risk to a greater extent than expected from the principal rules in articles 66 and 67: If the seller has committed a fundamental breach of contract, the buyer, according to article 70, still has the right to «the remedies available to the buyer on account of the breach», even if the risk has passed to him according to article 67, 68 and 69. A seller's fundamental breach of contract, such as serious delay or substantial lack of conformity of the goods, does not make it reasonable for the seller to be able to pass the consequences of accidental loss of or damage to the goods over to the buyer as soon as the seller has delivered the goods. However, if the loss or damage is due to the buyer's act or omission, the buyer nevertheless loses his right to declare the contract avoided, see article 82 (2) letter a).

For example: The sold engine has been handed over to the buyer, but when he tries to make use of it, it becomes obvious that the engine has a serious dysfunction beyond repair. If the lightning strikes the buyer's place of business the following night and the house where the engine is, burns down, article 82 (2) letter a) applies: The buyer may therefore still declare the contract avoided, even if he is not able to «make restitution of the goods substantially in the condition in which he received them» as required in article 82 (1).

3.16 Goods sold in transit.

Often the buyer decides to sell the goods before they arrive, while they are still under their way. This can safely be done by the use of shipping documents that represent the goods even if it is not present during transmission of the documents. In this new contract buyer, A, is seller and the new buyer, B, is buyer. In these situations article 68 decides at which time the risk passes to buyer B. The principal rule is that the risk passes to B at the time of the conclusion of the contract between A and B.

Since the second contract is made when the goods are under their way, perhaps on board a ship far away on the ocean, the contract parties do not have the possibility to inspect it. This situation raises questions whether the goods in that particular moment is in good shape or not. The goods may for example already be damaged by seawater. Who bears the risk then? It is not easy to decide whether the damage occurred before or after the contract of sale between A and B. The contract parties can avoid this problem by declaring that the risk is assumed by buyer B from the time the goods are handed over from the first seller to the carrier who issue the documents embodying the contract of carriage, see article 68, 2nd sentence.

In such a situation it is obviously important that the new contract parties, A and B, are fully honest and in good faith. Article 68, 3rd sentence declares: «Nevertheless, if at the time of the conclusion of the contract of sale the seller knew or ought to have known that the goods had been lost or damaged and did not disclose this to the buyer, the loss or damage is at the risk of the seller.» Article 7 also stresses the importance of «the observance of good faith in international trade».

3.17 Time of delivery, articles 33 and 34.

Earlier we have seen how far the goods have to be transported for them to be considered delivered. In this paragraph we will look at *when* this must have taken place in order to fulfil the contract, which means that delivery will not be considered delayed.

When we decide which date the goods should be delivered, we must first of all examine the contract, see article 33: «The seller must deliver the goods: (a) if a date is fixed by or determinable from the contract, on that date».

We will often find a fixed date stipulated in the contract. However, the contract is not always that clear. When the buyer sends an order to the seller, he normally expects delivery without any unnecessary delay.

If it is impossible to determine a date by examining the contract or by examining what has happened between the parties, we will have to rely on article 33 letter c): The seller must deliver the goods «within a reasonable time after the conclusion of the contract».

To explain what is *reasonable time,* we may find it useful to quote article 8 (3); «due consideration is to be given to all relevant circumstances of the case including the negotiations, any practices which the parties have established between themselves, usages and any subsequent conduct of the parties».

We will for example have to judge contracts for the supply of goods to be manufactured or produced (which may take its time) in a different manner than cases where the seller has (or ought to have had) the goods ready and handy in his warehouse.

In big manufacturing contracts, however, the day of delivery is normally stipulated in every detail in the contract. If we still have to rely on the term *reasonable time,* the situation itself will call for delivery without unnecessary delay.

Article 33 letter b) concerns cases where «a period of time is fixed by or determinable from the contract». In these cases the seller may deliver the goods «at any time within that period unless circumstances indicate that the buyer is to choose a date». The latter may be used in situations where the buyer for example needs some time to prepare necessary room for the goods.

According to article 34 the seller is bound to hand over the documents relating to the goods and see to it that the documents conform.

3.2 The obligation to pay the price

3.20 What price to pay?

The principal obligation of the seller is to pay the price, the contract sum, in due time.

The stipulation of the price is one of the most important parts of a contract. If the parties have not validly reached an agreement on the price, this may indicate that no contract is concluded, see CISG part II.

It is up to the parties do decide how the price is to be stipulated, for example referring to a particular index or price changes, like change of price from the seller's supplier. Terms like these are especially needed in cases where there is a period of time from contract formation until delivery. Price or cost indexes are particularly useful in contracts for the supply of goods to be manufactured or produced. This way the final determination of the price is postponed to the time of delivery. In big contracts the details concerning price can be rather complicated.

33

Even if the price is not in any way indicated, it may be extracted from a mutual understanding or understood by the circumstances that a particular price is meant, which often is the common market price. If the contract is simply concluded just when the seller fulfils the buyer's order, it is normally meant that the seller may use his ordinary price for the goods concerned. If this price differs too much from the market price, it may be difficult to construct a common understanding between the parties. We will then have to rely on article 55:

«Where a contract has been validly concluded but does not expressly or implicitly fix or make provision for determining the price, the parties are considered, in the absence of any indication to the contrary, to have impliedly made reference to the price generally charged at the time of the conclusion of the contract for such goods sold under comparable circumstances in the trade concerned.»

Article 55 will only apply where the contract «does not expressly or implicitly fix or make provision for determining the price». This article only applies if it is in fact the case that a contract has been validly concluded with such an important issue left out; see CISG part II about formation of the contract.

3.21 Place and time of payment.

«If the buyer is not bound to pay the price at any other particular place, he must pay it to the seller:
(a) at the seller's place of business; or
(b) if the payment is to be made against the handing over of the goods or of documents, at the place where the handing over takes place». See article 57 (1).

According to this, it is the buyer who has to see to it that the money arrives at the right place and in due time. He holds the risk of transmission of the money. If nothing else is indicated, the place of payment is the seller's place of business.

The safest way of payment is indicated in article 57 (1) letter b): The buyer does not need to pay before he has been handed over the goods or the documents. Also the other way around, the seller does not need to hand over the goods or the document, until he receives the payment. This is the classic payment on delivery situation. We see that this way both parties have a fair degree of guarantee; the seller can count the money and the buyer can examine the document or the goods, at least a preliminary examination.

The price is to be paid like an ordinary obligation to pay a sum of money, at the seller's place (article 57 (1) letter a)), which means that the money must be sent in time to reach the seller or the seller's bank account in due time. Since the money has to reach the seller (as prescribed in article 57 (1) letter a)), problems or delay during the transfer of money, is the buyer's risk. In case of delay the buyer will have to pay interest, see article 78. In more severe cases the seller may declare the contract avoided according to article 64. The seller cannot, however, claim damages (see article 61 (1) letter b)), if the buyer proves that the delayed payment «was due to an impediment beyond his control and that he could not reasonably be expected to have taken the impediment into account at the time of the conclusion of the contract or to have avoided or overcome it or its consequences», see article 79. This could be the case if there has been a stop of all transfer of money from the buyer's country or into the seller's country. This has to be a stop that could not have been foreseen or overcome.

As for the time of payment, article 58 (1) declares: «If the buyer is not bound to pay the price at any other specific time, he must pay it when the seller places either the goods or documents controlling their disposition at the buyer's disposal in accordance with the contract and this Convention. The seller may make such payment a condition for handing over the goods or documents.»

Here we see that it is, reasonably, up to the parties to agree on the time of payment. Article 58 applies when *no specific time is fixed*. When the seller has fulfilled his commitments, the buyer has to pay. Then the seller decides if he will accept delay – and how much, and the seller accordingly may set a fixed time within which the buyer has an obligation to pay. The seller may, however, decide that the buyer has to pay before the seller hands over the goods or documents, see article 58 (1) 2nd sentence.

3.3 Payment and delivery.

The principle of payment on delivery in article 58 is part of the general requirement of due balance in contracts and is a fundamental principle in the law of contract. Payment on delivery means that one contract party shall not be bound to fulfil his commitments under the contract unless his counterpart does the same.

The contract parties may nevertheless decide otherwise in their contract. The seller may deliver against a promise from the buyer to pay later, and the buyer sometimes accepts to pay the whole – or part of – the price before delivery. The latter may be necessary in order to supply the seller with funds to be able to manufacture the goods. If one of the parties has already fulfilled his obligations according to the contract, he has also given up his opportunity to suspend the performance of his own obligations if it then turns out that his counterpart does not perform, see article 71. Simply because at this time he has no longer any of his own obligations left to suspend.

Art 58, concerning payment on delivery, rests on these fundamental considerations:

1) *Security*. The right of a party (the buyer or the seller) to suspend his own performance may guarantee him against losses if the other party faces financial problems.

2) *Pressure*. When a party knows that he will not see the other party perform unless he performs himself, this will put pressure on him to try as hard as he can to perform his own obligations.

3) *Examination*. Especially for the buyer it is an advantage to be able to make an examination of the goods, even if it may only just be preliminary.

Chapter 4 Delivery of the goods

4.0 Breach of contract concerning delivery of the goods

4.00 Introduction.

Delayed or no delivery of the goods is a breach of contract by the seller, for not performing as required by the contract and article 30. We can divide delayed delivery into four categories:

1) The goods are delivered, but too late.

2) The goods are not delivered at all. They never arrive.

3) Floating delay: The time of delivery is exceeded, but the goods are not yet delivered. This situation will sooner or later materialise into one of the two types above; delayed delivery or no delivery.

4) Anticipatory breach. Even prior to the date of delivery, it becomes apparent that the seller is not going to deliver in time. See CISG articles 71 and 72 (paragraph 7.4 below).

The question of whether the seller has performed according to article 30 or not, will be decided by *examining and interpreting the contract* between the parties, the contract of sale. The contract may be clear or unclear dealing with this point, it may be oral or written, but either way we have to use the ordinary principles of contract interpretation of the law of contract, see also CISG article 8.

Normally the date of delivery in the contract means the *last* date the seller may deliver and still have fulfilled the contract. Some cases may occur in which delivery *prior to* the agreed date of delivery is to be considered a breach of contract; the goods, fresh flowers for instance, may be ordered for a special occasion. Now article 52 (1) applies: «If the seller delivers the goods before the date fixed, the buyer may take delivery or refuse to take delivery.»

If the contract does not specify a certain date of delivery, article 33 letter c) requires the seller to deliver the goods «within a reasonable time after the conclusion of the contract». What the word «reasonable» means, depends on the circumstances of each particular contract; type of goods, the buyer's place and the seller's place, means of transport, practices between the parties and usage in this particular type of business.

Breach of contract is committed if the seller does not deliver in due time. The breach consists of the gap between the seller's obligation and what he has actually managed to perform. When the date of delivery has come, and delivery has not taken place, we have a breach of contract. Whether the seller is to blame or not, or impediments have made correct delivery impossible, is irrelevant in this evaluation. Such facts may be of interest, though, when we decide which remedies the buyer is entitled to.

In some cases the contract has incorporated possible causes for delay in the contract's stipulated time of delivery. The effect of this is that the risk in the situations mentioned is transferred from the seller to the buyer: The seller, for instance, undertakes to deliver «as soon as possible after export licence is granted». Even if the governmental handling of the seller's application takes long or the application is rejected, we will have no breach of contract by the seller. In the same way the contract itself may depend on for instance adequate fish catch, fruit harvest or other such delicate and varying circumstances.

If the seller delivers on time, but the goods are so lacking in conformity that the buyer *refuses to take delivery*, we have a special kind of breach of contract. This breach may also be considered a delay because the goods, which are to be delivered on time, are goods conforming to the contract. This is particularly true for contracts for the supply of goods to be manufactured or produced: When the buyer refuses to take delivery of non conforming goods, the seller has to take the goods back and work on them until they match the contract. This is delayed delivery. In some cases, however, it is reasonable to look at the situation as remedying the lack of conformity by repair, see article 46 (3).

Deciding that a breach of contract by the seller has occurred is only the first part of the task. We must also decide *what rights the buyer can exercise* as a consequence of the breach of contract. These rights are called remedies for breach of contract.

It is easier to decide that delayed delivery is a breach of contract than to decide which remedies are available for the buyer as a compensation for this breach of contract.

A breach of contract is a minimum and necessary condition for the buyer to be entitled to remedies. See article 46 (1), the 1st sentence: «If the seller fails to perform any of his obligations under the contract or this Convention, the buyer may ...».

For each of the buyer's possible remedies we must also examine what other conditions must be filled. We will take a closer look at these in paragraph 4.1 below. They are not the same for all remedies, so we have to discuss each remedy separately.

CISG article 45 is an introductory article, like a table of content for the questions regulated in the following articles. In article 45 we find a list of the remedies, which may be available to the buyer for breach of contract by the seller:

    a) Exercise the rights provided in articles 46 to 52,
    b) Claim damages as provided in articles 74 to 77.

Now we have to take a closer look at the articles mentioned to see what conditions are connected to each particular remedy. For instance the buyer cannot declare the contract avoided simply because of a breach of contract by the seller; article 49 (1) goes on to declare that the breach has to be fundamental.

In certain cases the conditions for several remedies are met at the same time. Then the buyer may choose among these remedies. He may also be entitled to more than one remedy at a time. Thus he may require performance by the seller at the same time as he suspends his payment until delivery takes place and claims damages for losses caused by the failed delivery. The latter can be read out of article 45 (2): «The buyer is not deprived of any right he may have to claim damages by exercising his right to other remedies.» However, the buyer cannot declare the contract avoided at the same time as he requires performance, see article 46 (1). Avoidance is inconsistent with performance. He will first have to require performance, and then, if there is still no delivery in sight, he may declare the contract avoided.

4.1 Remedies for breach of contract obligation to deliver the goods

4.10 The buyer requires performance.

4.100 Introduction.

It is in fact a bit misleading to name the buyer's right to require delivery a remedy for breach of contract. Of course it is not necessary for the buyer to claim breach of contract in order to execute his right to require performance. This right follows directly from the contract and is what the whole contract is all about, whether there has been a breach of contract or not. That contract promises are to be kept is an important and fundamental principle of the law of contract. The idea of article 46 (1) is to make it clear that the buyer, even if the date of delivery is exceeded, still has the right to require the seller to deliver the goods (also called in natura) in stead of declaring the contract avoided. Often the buyer prefers to have the goods delivered even if they arrive so late that they are to be considered fundamentally delayed. The buyer does not always have a better alternative.

4.11 The buyer declares the contract avoided.

4.110 Introduction.

CISG article 49 concerns the buyer's right to declare the contract avoided.

Avoidance means that the contract shall have no effect, see article 81 (1): «Avoidance of the contract releases both parties from their obligations under it, subject to any damages which may be due.»

If the contract has already been performed – wholly or in parts – the goods delivered and the money paid under the contract, must be sent back to the other party, see article 81 (2).

In addition to declaring the contract avoided, the seller may claim damages as provided in articles 74 to 77: Now the buyer may, for instance, have to buy the goods from another seller and at a higher price. This is called a replacement transaction, and the price difference must be paid by the seller if the replacement order is placed «in a reasonable manner», see article 75.

4.111 Fundamental breach.

The principal condition that must be met before the buyer can declare the contract avoided, is that the delayed delivery «amounts to a fundamental breach of contract», article 49 (1) letter a). If there is no fundamental breach, the buyer may still claim damages according to articles 74 to 79, as we shall see in the next paragraph.

To decide if a delay amounts to a fundamental breach of the contract is not always an easy task.

Article 25: «A breach of contract committed by one of the parties is fundamental if it results in such detriment to the other party as substantially to deprive him of what he is entitled to expect under the contract, unless the party in breach did not foresee and a reasonable person of the same kind in the same circumstances would not have foreseen such a result».

We have to examine the contract, the delay and the circumstances. The delay in time must be held up against the problems the delay has caused the buyer. We must find out if these problems can be helped by other solutions and/or damage claims. The important term is what the buyer is «entitled to expect under the contract» (article 25). However, the buyer cannot declare the contract avoided if the seller «did not foresee and a reasonable person of the same kind in the same circumstances would not have foreseen such a result», see article 25.

Since the consideration here is complex, we cannot specify how many days (or weeks) are sufficient to amount to a fundamental breach. In some cases even hours will matter: The buyer has for instance ordered food, flowers or technical arrangements for a special event. If the buyer, under the negotiation prior to the contract formation, stressed the importance of having the goods present at a certain time, this will also point in the direction of fundamental breach: The manufacturer, who urgently needs raw materials for a new and very large order, explains to the seller why it is important that he receives the goods in due time.

The seller's conduct may effect whether the delay is fundamental or not. If the seller has been negligent or has given the buyer's order unreasonably low priority, this will count in the evaluation of the breach of contract. Even though negligence from the seller is no absolute condition to name the

43

delay fundamental, negligence is always a relevant fact, of lesser or greater importance depending on the circumstances of each individual case, which points towards fundamental breach. The seller's negligence is thus no absolute condition for the buyer to declare the contract avoided, but it does help.

4.112 Additional period of time. Notification.

According to article 49 (1) letter b) it matters whether or not the buyer has given the seller an additional period of time to deliver the goods. The buyer may declare the contract avoided if the seller does not deliver within this period of time or the seller declares that he will not deliver within the period of time the buyer has granted him. Here it is important to note, however, that the additional period of time fixed by the buyer has to be reasonable, see article 47 (1). It would not be fair to grant the buyer a right to avoidance if the delay is not fundamental as required in article 49 (1) letter a). The buyer cannot just allow a very short period of time in order to widen his right to declare the contract avoided. The term «fundamental breach of contract» in article 49 (1) letter a) is not very precise. Therefore the buyer is given this opportunity to try to fix the meaning of this term under the present individual contract by reasonably and loyally allowing an additional period of time of delivery.

This new period has to be definite and clear. It is not sufficient to express a wish that the goods be delivered as soon as possible.

A fixed additional period of time only influences the buyer's avoidance claim, see article 49. It does not affect the buyer's right to damages caused by the delayed delivery.

Granting the seller an additional period of time is mainly done when it has become likely that the goods will not be delivered on time. By fixing a period the buyer agrees not to declare the contract avoided if the seller manages to deliver within the fixed additional period. However, as mentioned, this does not influence other claims, for instance damages.

Article 48 (2) *enables the seller to take the initiative* by requesting «the buyer to make known whether he will accept performance» within a period of time *fixed by the seller*. When the buyer receives such a request, he must «comply with the request within a reasonable time». If the buyer does not answer, «the seller may perform within the time indicated in his request. The buyer may not, during that period of time, resort to any remedy which is inconsistent with performance by the seller» (article 48 (2)).

From this article we see that if the buyer does not react, he is not entitled to declare the contract avoided if the seller manage to deliver within the period of time the seller has granted himself for his own delayed delivery. Article 48 (2) gives the seller a chance to get rid of a troublesome uncertainty, even if the uncertainty is caused by the seller's own breach of contract. No reaction from the buyer in such a situation, gives the seller good reason to believe that the buyer wants delivery despite the delay. This is thus an exception from the general principle of the law of contract that a contract party cannot take the other party's silence for an accept.

The buyer may, however, claim damages from the seller if the delay causes him loss or expenditures, because claiming damages is *not* «inconsistent with performance by the seller», see article 48 (2).

It is important that the seller, in the same way that the buyer according to article 49 (1) letter b), remembers to fix a clear, precise and definite period of time. The seller may not just casually ask the buyer if he will accept some delay.

If the *seller has delivered the goods*, but the buyer still wants to declare the contract avoided because of fundamental delay, he must observe article 49 (2) letter a): The buyer has to declare the contract avoided «within a reasonable time after he has become aware that delivery has been made».

If an additional period of time has expired, regardless of it being fixed by the buyer according to article 47 (1) and 49 (1) or by the seller according to article 48 (2), the buyer must declare the contract avoided within a reasonable time. See the details in article 49 (2), where we in the last sentence see that it is not sufficient for the buyer to simply state that he will not accept performance. The declaration must be accompanied or followed by a definite declaration of avoidance.

4.12 The buyer claims damages.

4.120 Introduction. A main purpose behind articles 74 to 77 is compensation. This means that loss suffered by one contract party because of breach of contract by the other party is to be paid by the contract party in breach. When the seller delivers the goods too late – or does not deliver it at all – the buyer may claim damages according to these articles. Since the seller in this case is the party in breach, he is more likely to bear the costs of the breach than the buyer.

Another purpose behind damages is that of prevention. The articles aim to prevent breach of contract. A possible damages claim will stimulate the contract parties to try harder and to do their utmost to perform according to the contract and CISG. A party in possible breach will know that a breach of contract may have seriously negative consequences for him.

Articles 74 to 77 decide how the damages are to be calculated. These articles describe the kinds of loss to be included in the sum paid by the party who commits breach of contract. Here this means the sum the seller has to pay to the buyer as a consequence of the seller's breach of contract by delayed delivery.
First we have to examine article 79 concerning exemptions. If an exemption applies, the seller will not have to pay damages.

Therefore article 79 is the reasonable place to start when damages in sales contracts are to be discussed.

Article 79 exempts the seller from the liability to pay damages on certain occasions. Even though the seller does not have to pay damages in these cases, this does not prevent the buyer from «exercising any right other than to claim damages under this Convention», se article 79 (5). For example, if the delay amounts to a fundamental breach, the buyer is entitled to declare the contract avoided according to the regulations in article 49, even though an exemption in article 79 does apply.

4.121 Damages for breach of contract for delayed or no delivery.

Article 79 (1) declares that a party, in this case the seller, «is not liable for a failure to perform any of his obligations if he proves that the failure was due to an impediment beyond his control and that he could not reasonably be expected to have taken the impediment into account at the time of the conclusion of the contract or to have avoided or overcome it or its consequences.»

For the seller to avoid having to pay damages he has to meet four conditions according to article 79 (1):

The delay must be due to an impediment.
This impediment must lie beyond the seller's control.
The seller could not reasonably be expected to have taken the impediment into account at the time of the conclusion of the contract.
The seller could not reasonably be expected to have avoided or overcome the impediment or its consequences.

We must now take a closer look at these four conditions that have to be met if damages are to be avoided:

Especially on condition A, impediment. Real impediments make it impossible for the seller to manage to deliver the goods. A typical example is when the contract concerns a special item, a used car. If the car is stolen or totally damaged, it is not possible for the seller to perform according to the contract. Another example is where the whole lot from which the goods are to be taken is destroyed. Other examples are import or export prohibition or ban on the sale of the product in question. The given circumstances make it impossible for the seller to perform according to the contract. This is in accordance with an old roman principle, *impossibilium nulla est obligatio.*

Condition C in article 79 (1) requires the seller to «overcome the impediment or its consequences»: If it turns out that the contract can not be performed in the way the seller had expected, he has to try other solutions: If the seller's regular supplier fails to deliver, the seller must search around for other suppliers. This applies even if a new supplier is more expensive. The seller himself is responsible for his calculations and must accept a loss if they do not hold. The seller, who has committed himself to a contract, has to perform according to it even if that means working harder and paying more than he expected.

In some cases, however, the contract is written in such detail that there is no alternative way to perform it: A contract may, for instance, require five tons Kerrs Pink potatoes from West Hill farm. If the whole crop here is damaged, it is impossible to deliver according to the contract. It would have been different if the contract had not specified which farm the potatoes were to be taken from. In that case the seller would have had to get hold on the potatoes elsewhere. We thus see that the way in which the contract is written, decides which limits the seller has to act within. The greater freedom the contract offers, the harder the seller has to work to perform delivery. The seller is required to perform according to the contract, but he neither has a commitment nor a right to deliver anything else.

Expensive impediments. The principal rule is that the seller still has the obligation to deliver the goods, even if delivery turns out to be more expensive and more demanding than expected. The seller cannot claim this as an impediment. Nevertheless, we must also look at condition D earlier in article 79 (1) and read both condition A and condition D. The question will then be if the seller could «reasonably be expected to ... overcome the impediment or its consequences». It is a well-known fact that money can some times make the impossible possible. But how much money can we reasonably expect the seller to spend in order to overcome the impediments and manage to deliver the goods? This is not an easy decision to make. Condition C will also have a say in this: It is here a question of impediments, which the seller «could not reasonably be expected to have taken the impediment into account at the time of the conclusion of the contract». All conditions A to D, including C, have to be met if the seller shall avoid the buyer's claim for damages. If the seller cannot be blamed for not having foreseen the trouble, it may be unreasonable to ask him to spend amounts of money that will render the contract unprofitable.

Obviously a certain delay is likely to occur in some cases: For instance; the ship with the goods on board is grounded and the goods are lost just hours before the ship should have reached the buyer's port where delivery according to the contract was to take place. It is now impossible for the seller to deliver in time. We cannot require him to have ordered one extra ship, just in case. However, the seller does have to dispatch undamaged goods as soon as possible and in this way overcome the impediment.

Especially on condition B, beyond control. Here we have to separate circumstances beyond the seller's control from circumstances within his control. If the seller or his employees have not acted the way they should, in other words negligence on the side of the seller, this lies within the seller's control: The seller's employees have, for instance, made mistakes during the manufacturing or the seller has not instructed his workers well enough. On the other hand, circumstances that are no one's fault may still lie within the seller's control. The term «beyond control» does not point to a negligence or culpa decision. We may therefore reasonably use the term *the seller's sphere of control*. This is circumstances that the seller in principle is able to control, whether he is to blame or not, provided it is an area he can influence. If the seller's factory burns down due to an accident during work or dysfunction in the electric system, it lies within the seller's sphere of control, even if no one is to blame. The seller is therefore liable if he fails to deliver in due time because of the fire. If, however, the factory burns down due to the supplier of electricity or is struck by lightning, this impediment lies beyond the seller's control.

Another example is problems in the seller's financial situation. The seller may not be to blame for the situation, for example when his other customers have not paid in time for the goods the seller has delivered to them. The seller is still liable if he due to a weak financial position is not able to deliver the goods according to the contract.

A strike, which is limited to the seller's factory, may in some cases be reasonable consider an event within the seller's control. The result is liability if the seller does not deliver in time. This may seem somewhat harsh on the seller, and he will possibly be exempt if he has done what he reasonably could to avoid the strike. On the other hand, a nation wide strike is beyond the seller's control exempting him from liability according to article 79.

On condition C, taking the impediment into account. Even if an impediment is beyond the seller's control he may still be liable for the delayed delivery. This will be the case if the seller *could* «reasonably be expected to have taken the impediment into account at the time of the conclusion of the contract», se article 79 (1) condition C. Contrary to condition A and B, by the term «reasonably be expected» this article openly signalises that we shall consider if there is culpa or negligence on the side of the seller. The question is if it is reasonable to require the seller to be more foresighted: If an export ban was already known when the contract was made, the seller is liable when this impediment causes the seller's failure to perform in due time. An export ban could also be unexpected: The authorities may, for instance, have done their best to keep it a secret before it is made public. In the latter case the seller is not liable for failure to deliver if he cannot overcome the impediment for instance by applying for a dispensation from the new export ban.

On the other hand, the seller must not forget to observe article 79 (4) and accordingly give the buyer «notice ... of the impediment and its effect on his ability to perform». If the seller fails to notify the buyer, it may be of little importance that he avoids liability according to article 79 (1), since he is now liable for the kind of damages described in article 79 (4): «If the notice is not received by the other party within a reasonable time after the party who fails to perform knew or ought to have known of the impediment, he is liable for damages resulting from such non-receipt.»

The seller is not, however, the only contract party who has to take possible impediments into account. Import restrictions, for instance, will in most cases be easier for *the buyer* to foresee, since this is regulation originated in his country. Therefore the seller may be exempt from liability – given the other conditions in article 79 (1) are met – if an import ban or import regulations prohibit or delay the delivery of the goods. This also goes for cases where the buyer has instructed the seller from which particular supplier the seller is to order materials needed for the manufacturing of the goods, and this supplier fails to deliver in due time. In other cases the seller himself is liable for failure by his supplier – or for failure by a third person which services the seller relies on, see article 79 (2).

In such cases we must decide if the seller could reasonably be expected to take into account circumstances like extremely bad weather or unfrozen/frozen waters, failing fisheries or extraordinarily bad harvest. These are often difficult decisions to make. Therefore it is highly recommended that the seller demand exemption concerning such extreme circumstances written into the contract itself, especially if he is in a business where delicate factors influence the possibility of delivering the goods. Extreme conditions may hit the seller hard. For a fishing company: It will be bad enough for this company first to be hit by the failing fisheries and the subsequent diminished incomes in themselves, if it should not be met with damage claims from his buyers. The buyers do not risk that much, because they are not committed to pay for fish that never arrive, see article 49. They can use their money to order fish elsewhere (or try to persuade their customers to eat something else).

*On condition D, avoid or overcome the impediment.*Even if an impediment should lie beyond the seller's control, and even if he could not reasonably be expected to have taken it into account at the time of the conclusion of the contract (conditions A, B and C are thus met), he could still be liable. According to condition D of article 79 (1), it may be reasonable to expect him to overcome the impediment or its consequences. If the seller has not done enough in this respect, the buyer may claim damages. The seller could perhaps have overcome the consequences of lack of raw materials by having stored a sufficient reserve. If it is a question of export restrictions it might have been possible to apply for a dispensation or an export licence. If one supplier of raw materials fails, the sufficient materials might be ordered elsewhere. The crucial question is how much «can be reasonably expected» of the seller, and this must be answered in each particular case. As long as the seller has committed himself to a contract, it is to be expected that he actually fulfils his obligations. If this turns out to be more expensive or difficult than he expected when he concluded the contract, this is on its own no reason to make exemption from the seller's liability. It is the seller's own task to calculate correctly and to foresee (or guess for that sake) the development in the relevant markets for raw materials. This is the seller's homework, so to speak.

We cannot exclude, however, that on certain occasions it may be so expensive or difficult to deliver that the seller according to article 79 (1) «could not reasonably be expected ... to have avoided or overcome the impediment or its consequences». Here we have a close connection between condition A and condition D, as we saw when we discussed condition A above: Whether an impediment actually is to be considered a relevant impediment will naturally depend on how hard it is to overcome it.

4.122 Delayed delivery due to a third person.

On some occasions the seller fails to deliver the goods in time because of a third person, which assists the seller during the performance of his obligations. If the seller has carelessly decided which third person to rely on, he will not avoid liability according to article 79 (1), because this is of course within his own control. The seller chooses for instance a third person that does not possess the necessary experience or skill to manage the task given to him. On many occasions the seller ought to have known this or at least ought to have examined the third person more carefully. The same is likely to be the case if the seller has instructed the third person badly or given him inferior drawings.

Even if none of the instances mentioned above is the case, and the seller therefore according to article 79 (1) is not liable for his failure to deliver in time, he may still be liable according to article 79 (2). The purpose of the 2nd paragraph of article 79 is to avoid that the seller successfully escapes liability by blaming a third person. The third person may have such an independent position that the seller cannot influence his work, instruct him or tell him what to do. Here we have to say that the third person's failure and delay lies beyond the seller's control. This tends to make the seller *not* liable according to article *79 (1)*. In these cases we see that article *79 (2)* is necessary in order to make the seller liable for the fact that his buyer does not receive his goods on time.

Article 79 (2): «If the party's failure is due to the failure by a third person whom he has engaged to perform the whole or a part of the contract, that party is exempt from liability only if:
(a) he is exempt under the preceding paragraph; and
(b) the person whom he has so engaged would be so exempt if the provisions of that paragraph were applied to him».

Note the word «*and*» connecting letter a) and letter b): *Both* the seller *and* the third person he has engaged have to be exempt under article 79 (1). Both of them must have been struck by a relevant impediment. This is sometimes called «double force majeure». Seen from the seller's point of view paragraph 2 in article 79 widens his liability: It is not sufficient for the seller himself to be exempt according to article 79 (1). It will be of no help to the seller unless the third person as well is exempt according to the same article 79 (1). See article 79 (2), letter b).

According to this we may say that the conditions A to D earlier in article 79 (1) has to be met twice; first the seller himself has to meet all the four conditions, then the third person in question has to meet the same four conditions. We have a total of eight checkpoints all of which have to be met. If there is failure in passing just one of these eight checkpoints the seller is not exempt from the buyer's claim of damages.

The seller shall not, as we have seen, be exempt from his liability towards the buyer by transferring the performance of the contract partly or as a whole to a third person, and eventually blame the third person if something goes wrong.

This does not mean, however, that the third person has no liability what so ever. The seller may, if he has paid damages to the buyer, claim his money back from the third person because of the latter's breach of contract. This new claim is to be decided according to the contract between the seller and the third person. It may also be possible for the buyer to raise claims against the third person, which the buyer may prefer to do if the seller lacks the will and/or ability to pay damages.

By the term «third person» article 79 (2) refers to a «person whom he [the seller] has engaged to perform the whole or a part of the contract». This term includes anyone who assists the seller during his performance of his obligation under the contract. This could be the person who manufactures a certain component needed in a big machine, which the seller is to deliver, the person who transports the goods to the buyer, or the person who installs the delivered machinery in the buyer's factory.

Let us here stress that article 79 (2) says that *the seller* must have engaged the third person. This means that the seller himself chooses to make use of this particular third person and his services. If the buyer has reserved the right to decide which third person to engage, article 79 (2) will not apply. This is reasonably also the case if there is in fact only one third-person that can possibly be engaged, for instance the general supplier of water or electricity.

4.123 Liability for temporary impediments.

When the seller is provided exemption by article 79 (1) and (2), this exemption «has effect for the period during which the impediment exists», see article 79 (3). If the impediment ceases to exist, the exemption no longer has any effect, which means that the seller from now on is liable if he does not take steps to fulfil delivery. We must examine the case and find out whether or not the seller may still call upon article 79 (1). The elapsed time may make it unreasonable to expect the seller to be ready to deliver at any time. If the goods no longer exist when the export ban is eventually lifted, this means there is a new impediment.

4.124 Notification of impediment.

If the seller fails to perform, he must give notice to the buyer «of the impediment and its effect on his ability to perform», see article 79 (4) that continues as follows: «If the notice is not received by the other party within a reasonable time after the party who fails to perform knew or ought to have known of the impediment, he is liable for damages resulting from such non-receipt.» This kind of liability is independent from CISG's other articles concerning damages. Even if the seller is exempt from liability because of a relevant impediment according to article 79 (1), he could still be liable according to article 79 (4).

The calculation of damages is different from the ordinary articles on calculation (articles 74 to 77). According to article 79 (4), the seller is only liable for damages resulting from non-receipt of notification. The seller is only liable for the loss that the buyer could have avoided if he had received notification of the delayed delivery. If the buyer had received notification he might have been able to arrange for an alternative solution; for instance, the buyer could have maintained his old machinery or hired another machine for a period of time until the delayed machinery arrived from the seller. If he had received due notification, the buyer might have been able to reduce his loss this way. The seller is therefore liable for the cost difference. If the seller is *not* liable according to this paragraph, he is accordingly not at all liable for damages, if he because of the impediment is exempt by article 79 (1).

If the seller *is not exempt* according to article 79 (1), he is liable whether he notifies the buyer or not. It is however still recommended that he notify the buyer of the delayed delivery. When the buyer receives such notification, he is, according to article 77, required «to mitigate the loss, including loss of profit, resulting from the breach. If he fails to take such measures, the party in breach may claim a reduction in the damages in the amount by which the loss should have been mitigated». So we see that even if the seller is liable according to article 79 (1), he could be able to reduce the damages he will have to pay, by notifying the buyer and thus making the buyer take steps to reduce his loss caused by the delayed delivery.

Chapter 5. Conformity of the goods

Breach of Contract by lack of conformity

5.0 What is lack of conformity according to the CISG?

5.00 Introduction. Our discussion of CISG's articles concerning lack of conformity with the contract is divided into two parts: First we will discuss situations where the goods do not conform with the contract. Then (paragraph 5.1) we will discuss the consequences of lack of conformity. If the goods do not conform, the buyer may exercise rights according to articles 45 to 52 of the CISG, see article 45. Non-conformity is the main condition for the buyer to be able to execute such rights. Other conditions must be discussed for each particular sanction the buyer may execute.

We will finally mention a special kind of breach; third party claims (paragraph 5.2 below).

5.01 To read the contract is the first step.

The first thing to do is to compare the delivered goods to the contract between the seller and the buyer. This is the principal point when deciding on lack of conformity, see article 35 (1):

«The seller must deliver goods which are of the quantity, quality and description required by the contract and which are contained or packaged in the manner required by the contract.»

It is up to the contract parties to decide whether to make a contract or not, what goods to be delivered; of first quality, standard quality or even bad quality. This is a question of interpreting a contract. Here the ordinary principles of the law of contract apply, see also CISG article 8.

There are considerable differences within the sales contracts as to how detailed and thoroughly the goods are described. Some contracts are very detailed and comprehensive, especially contracts for the supply of goods to be manufactured or produced. If big values are at stake the contract is likely to contain very detailed descriptions and drawings of the product to be delivered. This is of course of great importance to the conformity evaluation, which generally will consist of comparing the goods delivered to the requirements found in the contract. We may presume that a very detailed and carefully formed contract is meant to be comprehensive in its description of the goods: If the buyer then claims that the goods should meet criteria which are not mentioned in the contract, he may not be heard in cases where the contract is very detailed. Some contracts contain a so-called «entire contract» paragraph, which means that only criteria directly mentioned in the contract apply.

Many contracts are in the other end of the scale though: The buyer needs the goods as soon as possible, and does not want to take the time to agree on a detailed description in a written contract. The goods in question might be standardized or he trusts that the seller understands what is needed. In such cases the oral agreement, for instance by telephone, is often very simple and informal. Here the contract has to be accompanied by other available information, like advertisements, brochures, information on the package and instructions for use or warranty documents. If the information available is scarce, we may have to assume that ordinary and reasonable quality, which is generally accepted in the market, is meant.

5.02 The purpose of the contract.

An important factor when deciding on conformity of the goods is to look at the buyer's motive; why did he buy these things? This is often obvious: A chair should be able to carry the weight of an adult person, a watch should show the correct time, and raincoats must yield protection against rain. If the things cannot be used for normal purposes, they do not conform. CISG article 35 (2) states: «Except where the parties have agreed otherwise, the goods do not conform with the contract unless they: (a) are fit for the purposes for which goods of the same description would ordinarily be used».

Even if the price is low, certain basic requirements must be met. Where the parties have not agreed otherwise or there are other clues pointing in different directions, we can assume that the buyer has ordinary motives for making the contract.

In some cases the goods *do conform* even if they are *not* fit for the purposes for which goods of the same description would ordinarily be used. If the buyer has bought a lot of wooden chairs to burn for heating, he cannot complain if they break down during ordinary use. This is also the case when the racehorse is sold for meat or the breads are meant for pig feeding. In such cases other circumstances may also be of interest; the price fixed in the contract will indicate if the buyer has actually meant to use the goods in the ways just mentioned.

The above examples concern cases where the buyer cannot expect very much from the goods. On certain occasions, however, the buyer may have needs well beyond ordinary purposes or in another direction: The buyer's expectations for the goods go beyond «the purposes for which goods of the same description would ordinarily be used», as expressed in article 35 (2) letter a). The buyer's particular need is therefore not ordinary. On the contrary; it is extraordinary and therefore applied to by article 35 (2) *letter b)* stating that the goods do not conform if non-ordinary requirements are not met:

«Except where the parties have agreed otherwise, the goods do not conform with the contract unless they: ...
(b) are fit for any particular purpose expressly or impliedly made known to the seller at the time of the conclusion of the contract, except where the circumstances show that the buyer

did not rely, or that it was unreasonable for him to rely, on the seller's skill and judgement».

From carefully reading this paragraph we see that for the buyer to claim that the goods do not conform, two conditions have to be met; visibility and skill.

1) Visibility: *The buyer's purpose must be visible to the seller*: It must «expressly or impliedly [be] made known to the seller at the time of the conclusion of the contract».

2) Skill: *The seller must possess skill*, and the circumstances must also give the buyer reasons to rely on the seller's skill and judgement.

Article 35 (2) *letter b)* mainly applies to cases where the buyer presents his less ordinary purpose to the seller asking him for advice based on the seller's skill and judgement. The paragraph does not require the buyer's purpose to be made known expressly: The buyer's purpose can be made known «impliedly», as it says. This means that the purpose must be visible to the seller; it must have been possible for the seller to notice it. Further it must be reasonable to expect the seller to notice it, even if he in this particular case actually did not. How obvious the buyer's purpose should be in order to have been «impliedly made known» to the seller, is not always easy to decide. We must find a certain amount of negligence from the side of the seller for him to be liable.

The buyer's purpose should be obvious and visible in such a degree that the seller «could not have been unaware» of it, which is how CISG article 40, in another connection, expresses the seller's negligence (as to examine the goods). It is not sufficient that the seller ought to have known the buyer's purpose.

CISG article 35 (2), letter b) applies directly to one type of situation, and that situation is regarded as lack of conformity.

But what about all the cases concerning unusual purposes which are not covered by this paragraph? For example when the buyer does not rely on – or cannot rely on – the seller's skill and judgement, or the seller *could* reasonably be unaware of the buyer's purpose. Then we have lack of skill or lack of visibility – or both. The CISG does not solve this question. We can then assume that the buyer does not have any legal basis for claims against the seller. The buyer himself must then bear the risk of his extraordinary purpose, which he has not managed to convey visibly to the seller. If the goods fail to function the way the buyer expected them to, the buyer will be the party most likely to bear the costs caused by this failure; provided the conditions in article 35 (2) letter b) are not met.

From this we see that a contract party must carry the risk of his own expectations when he has failed to make them visible to the other contract party.

We may not, however, draw the opposite conclusion and state lack of conformity if the goods do not meet a *visible* non-ordinary purpose. An example will show that the seller is not always liable even if he knows the buyer's special purpose: If an oil company buys some bags of marble balls from a toy factory to use in oil drilling, it will be the oil company's loss if the balls do not function the way the company had expected. Even if the toy factory was thoroughly briefed on the processes in which the marble balls were to be used, the factory will not be liable if the plan does not work. Here the seller lacks the skill, which is required in article 35 (2), letter b). On the contrary, the buyer possesses – or was supposed to have possessed – the necessary technical skill. It is reasonable to ask which party has the best insight in the process in which the goods are to be used. If both parties are equally skilled in the area concerned – or both are without any particular skill – the decision may be more difficult. We should then recognize that we are discussing an extraordinary purpose, and then as a consequence of that make the buyer carry the risk of his purpose. A general principle of the law of contract is that a contract party carries the risk of his own purposes.

A particular case occurs when the goods are to be used as raw materials for developing and manufacturing a brand new product. Even if it is a new product, we cannot really consider it an extraordinary use. Nevertheless it seems reasonable that the party (here the buyer), who develops a new product, carries the risk when both parties possess more or less the same level of skill. Since the buyer is the one to benefit if the new product succeeds, he should accordingly carry the losses in case of failure.

5.03 Price and quality.

It is obvious that the price is an important point in the conformity consideration. The contract of sale should normally be understood in a way in which the parties' mutual *obligations are reasonably balanced*, that there is balance between the price to pay and the goods to be delivered.

If the sale concerns a second hand machine at a price of 200 000, it is much easier for the buyer to claim lack of conformity by substantial corrosion than it would be if the price was 5 000. In the latter example the price should make the buyer adjust his expectations as to the quality of the machine. New mass manufactured goods should be dealt with in the same way. We often find considerable differences in quality between the various product brands. Some watches are more precise than others. Some car models are better protected against corrosion than competing models, which again may benefit from better driving properties. We cannot normally name such differences in quality lack of conformity. The fact that cheap watches with a sale price of 10 are not as good as watches at a price of 100 must of course be accepted. It might be lack of conformity, however, if the more expensive watches are not better than the cheaper ones in this example. But we cannot always expect a millimetre conformance between price and quality.

In newspapers and magazines we often find various product tests, and the most expensive model is not always «best in test». In many cases one model may have both plusses and minuses: One car may possess a strong and durable motor, while the resistance against corrosion is weaker. The latter will not be named lack of conformity. The individual factory must be granted a certain amount of freedom to choose what specific product it wishes to offer its customers. Some companies spend a lot of money to protect its cars from corrosion while the competitors work harder on the motor's duration. This explains why the cheaper car may be better protected against corrosion. This fact alone, however, will not give the buyer reason to complain about the more expensive model.

5.04 Time for judgment on conformity.

For the seller to be liable for lack of conformity, this lack must exist «at the time when the risk passes to the buyer, even though the lack of conformity becomes apparent only after that time», see article 36 (1). The time for the passing of risk is to be decided according to articles 66 to 70 (see paragraph 3.1 earlier in this book): The risk normally passes to the buyer when the goods are delivered. The lack of conformity has to be present at this time. This does not mean, however, that it has to be discovered at this time. Hidden faults are in many cases not discovered until a considerable period of time after delivery. The buyer may still raise claims, provided he does not fail to give the seller notice of this lack of conformity according to article 39 (1) «within a reasonable time after he has discovered it or ought to have discovered it».

Article 36 (1) may raise difficult issues concerning proof. A claim often fails because there is not sufficient proof of lack of conformity being present when the goods are delivered. Examples of fault existing already on delivery of the goods, are manufacturing faults and use of bad raw materials during manufacturing, for instance low sustainability. On the other hand we have breakdowns caused by wrong usage, lack of maintenance, influence from outside (corrosion, accident) or wear and tear. In these latter cases the goods may have been conforming at the time of delivery. But not necessarily: Failures by wear and tear may have been caused by inferior raw materials used in the production. These raw materials were already bad at the time of delivery: If an expensive quality watch stops after just one year of normal use because of wear and tear, this is a clear sign of lack of conformity with the contract. This will not necessarily be the case if a watch is sold at a very low price without any such quality promises from the seller. In the latter case cheap raw materials may be an important factor in keeping the production costs, and thereby the price, at a low level.

Instructions for use. Bad functioning caused by accidents or the wrong use is according to article 36 (1) not to be considered lack of conformity. It would be different if there were errors in the instructions, and these errors led to wrong use. Such insufficient guidance may be considered a breach of contract. See article 36 (2) which makes the seller «liable for any lack of conformity which occurs after the time indicated in the preceding paragraph and which is due to a breach of any of his obligations». Even if in this particular case the goods alone may conform, the seller's total performance will not conform if the instructions are not good enough.

To decide on lack of conformity is a difficult task, especially when some period of time has elapsed since the goods were delivered. Some of the problems concerning proof may be eliminated if in the contract the parties have already agreed on which specific and stipulated faults/problems the buyer may react on by requesting repair or making other claims for breach of contract. This is quite a widespread method of contract formation, and it may take the form of a guarantee:

Also see article 36 (2), which makes the seller liable for lack of conformity «which is due to a breach of any of his obligations, including a breach of any guarantee that for a period of time the goods will remain fit for their ordinary purpose or for some particular purpose or will retain specified qualities or characteristics». In order to decide *which specific* purpose, qualities or characteristics the seller guarantees we have to closely examine and interpret the contract and the relevant circumstances from the contract formation process.

In general the buyer has a strong case if he is capable of discovering the lack of conformity immediately after delivery has been made. If, however, a substantial period of time elapses before discovery, it is much easier for the seller to claim that the lack of conformity is due to wrong usage, wear and tear, corrosion, lack of maintenance, influence from outside or any other reason that does not represent lack of conformity with the contract.

CISG article 36 (2) makes an exception from the principal rule in article 36 (1) for cases where the lack of conformity is due to a breach of any of the seller's obligations: The seller is still liable for lack of conformity that occurs *after delivery* if he has not fulfilled his obligations under the contract: For instance, the goods have been packed so badly that it has resulted in transport damages, or the seller or his assistants made mistakes during installation at the buyer's place of business.

5.05 Longevity of the goods.

We have all discovered the simple truth that there are great differences as to how well goods function as time goes by. Not many products last forever. A product's longevity is seldom very precisely stipulated by the seller. To stipulate this is not an easy task. Often the contract parties address these questions *by agreeing in the contract* that the seller guarantees the goods for a certain period of time, for instance three months or up to two years or even several years in some cases. Thereby both parties know exactly what they can rely on. The goods will hopefully last substantially longer than the stipulated guaranteed period of time. But after this period faults and malfunctions are statistically so numerous that it would be much too costly for the seller to undertake liability for a longer period of time, without increasing the price. An agreement on guarantee is often differentiated in such a way that certain components are guaranteed for a long time, while others for a shorter period of time. Some components may not be guaranteed at all. New cars, for instance, may be sold with a general guarantee of *one year*, but with *six years* against corrosion and only *six months* for short lasting particles.

If the contract parties have not made stipulations of any kind, the CISG article 39 (2) applies:

«In any event, the buyer loses the right to rely on a lack of conformity of the goods if he does not give the seller notice thereof at the latest within a period of two years from the date on which the goods were actually handed over to the buyer, unless this time-limit is inconsistent with a contractual period of guarantee».

Certain objects cannot be expected to last very long. Therefore lack of conformity cannot always be claimed even if the product stops functioning after a relatively *short period of time*:

A light bulb is not necessarily defective even if it goes out after some months of use, and thus does not last the two years indicated in article 39 (2) as the limit for notification. This is also true for the cheapest watches.

In general we must accept accidental differences in longevity between individual items, even within the same brand. However, manufacturing faults and other real lacks of conformity cannot be accepted.

It is, of course, fully legal to manufacture goods with short longevity. Various cheap articles are made from materials possessing little wear resistance, thus the product may not last long. If a customer needs a special type of screwdriver and only plans to use it one time or two, he may be perfectly satisfied with the cheapest alternative. However, if the screwdriver is meant for intensive professional use, the buyer may save costs in the end by choosing the best, even if it is also the most expensive.

The seller must not market his product in a way that gives the buyer unrealistic expectations of high quality and longevity. The buyer will then often be able to claim lack of conformity according to the CISG article 35. In addition to the contract itself, the marketing and the information given by the seller, *the price* will be a crucial factor when deciding if the goods lack conformity.

What we have to interpret is not only the contract itself, but also the whole contract situation; see articles 8 and 9 concerning intentions, usage and practice. If the particular parties are regular business partners, former contracts will be relevant, because in such cases a lot will be assumed and not mentioned expressly. Everything that might shed light on what the parties once agreed upon will be of interest.

Each of the parties must prove the facts, which he claims. For instance if the buyer claims that the seller has orally guaranteed a certain use, the buyer must be able to prove the likeliness of this fact. Both oral and written information from the seller is relevant, but the buyer makes his case easier if he has something written to show to.

It is obvious that the seller is liable for any information he has personally given. Information may also have been given *by others on behalf of the seller*. The question is then whether the person who has given the information is actually in a position to act on behalf of the seller.

5.06 The goods' accordance with a sample or model.

If the seller has sent the buyer products «as a sample or model», the CISG article 35 (2) letter c) states that the actual goods ordered must possess the same quality when delivered. We have to look into why the buyer has required (or the seller offered) goods «as a sample or model» since this is of importance for the judgment on the buyer's examination of the goods and possible negligence, see below.

5.07 The buyer's examination of the goods. Negligence.

The CISG article 35 (3) declares:

«The seller is not liable under subparagraphs (a) to (d) of the preceding paragraph for any lack of conformity of the goods if at the time of the conclusion of the contract the buyer knew or could not have been unaware of such lack of conformity».

This is a description of a relatively severe negligence by the buyer; he «knew or could not have been unaware of such lack of conformity» and this is clearly a more severe negligence than if the article had said just «ought to have known». If the buyer only ought to have known about the lack of conformity, he has been a bit careless and should have been more careful, but this is not sufficient to exempt the seller from his liability. For the seller to be exempt according to article 35 (3), the buyer must have been more careless than that, and there must be reasons to criticise him more severely for his greater negligence and his obvious lack of attention. Article 35 (3) refers to «the time of the conclusion of the contract» and does not require the buyer to examine the goods at this early stage. If in fact the buyer is given the opportunity to examine the goods (or a sample or model, see article 35 (2) letter c)), this will naturally influence what the buyer «knew or could not have been unaware of».

We have to stress that the seller, too, may have been negligent. See article 40, which declares that the «seller is not entitled to rely on the provisions of articles 38 and 39 if the lack of conformity relates to facts of which he knew or could not have been unaware and which he did not disclose to the buyer».

We see that the same term is used here as in article 35 (3). Thus the same degree of relatively severe negligence is meant in both paragraphs.

If the goods lack conformity according to *article 35 (2)*, the seller is, according to article 35 (3), not liable if «the buyer knew or could not have been unaware of such lack of conformity». If the goods, however, lack conformity according to *article 35 (1)*, article 35 (3) does not apply, as the latter paragraph limits itself to article 35 (2). According to article 40 the seller is liable «if the lack of conformity relates to facts of which he knew or could not have been unaware and which he did not disclose to the buyer», even if the buyer fails to notify the seller according to articles 38 and 39.

If both parties, the seller and the buyer, «knew or could not have been unaware of» the goods' lack of conformity, the seller *is* liable for such lack of conformity as described in article 35 (1), but *not* for such described in article 35 (2). Read article 40 and article 35 (3) respectively.

The distinctions are not quite easy to grasp, especially since there is no clear-cut border between paragraphs (1) and (2) of article 35. Perhaps we may try to distinguish the case by asking if one of the parties seems to be more to blame than the other party. If the seller has knowingly failed to disclose to the buyer a lack of conformity, while the buyer has «only» been severely negligent (he could not have been unaware of the lack), the seller is more responsible and should thus be liable. If the buyer is the one who has been the most to blame the tables will turn. Which party was most likely to discover the fault in the goods? Who possesses the skill necessary to discover it? Should any of the parties have taken the initiative to seek help from experts? These and other such questions may contribute to place the risk of fault discovery with one of the contract parties. Again we refer to article 8 (3), which in general gives consideration «to all relevant circumstances of the case including the negotiations, any practices which the parties have established between themselves, usages and any subsequent conduct of the parties».

When the goods are eventually delivered, the CISG article 38 (1) requires the buyer to «examine the goods, or cause them to be examined, within as short a period as is practicable in the circumstances». This paragraph does not, however, state exactly *when* this examination is to take place. It seems clear that the buyer should not postpone it. We see that the period is «short», and the question is what «is practicable in the circumstances». The buyer is not always allowed to wait until delivery, if he is given practical opportunities to examine the goods earlier, for example if the seller gives the buyer the opportunity to make a sufficient examination already during the contract formation, provided the goods are available.

Some guidance is given in article 38 (2): «If the contract involves carriage of the goods, examination may be deferred until after the goods have arrived at their destination». As we see, the buyer may wait till the goods have arrived, but it is clearly stated that he can not wait any longer than that, provided examination is «practicable» according to the first paragraph in article 38.

When loading and unloading the goods the transport company regularly examines the packages to uncover possible damages.

Article 38 (1) does not state exactly *how* the examination is to be undertaken. Practices and usages are relevant, as well as other circumstances generally described in article 8 (3). If the seller has given information and further specifications concerning the goods, the buyer should be able to rely on them. The buyer will not have to check or double check such information from the seller unless there are obvious reasons for doubt.

How skilled the buyer's examination should be, depends on how skilled he is as a buyer. We expect more from an expert in the particular field, than from one with ordinary qualifications. The buyer does not need to undertake the examination personally. That article 38 (1) says «or cause them to be examined» will be of interest when the buyer is away and has to rely on others to have the goods examined. Does this mean that the buyer has to hire experts to examine the goods? Probably not. To hire experts may be extremely costly. The CISG should have expressed it more clearly if the intention was to require a less experienced or skilled buyer to hire experts to examine the goods. The buyer will often hire an expert in his own interest: Even if the seller may be liable for lack of conformity, it is important for the buyer to have knowledge thereof as soon as possible to be able to clear the situation without delay. By acting quickly the buyer may be able to avoid both inconvenience and losses later on.

During transport, especially if several means of transport are relied on and the goods are redirected, it can be difficult to decide where to undertake the examination of the goods. In this case the «examination may be deferred until after the goods have arrived at the new destination», see paragraph (3) in article 38:

«If the goods are redirected in transit or redispatched by the buyer without a reasonable opportunity for examination by him and at the time of the conclusion of the contract the seller knew or ought to have known of the possibility of such redirection or redispatch, examination may be deferred until after the goods have arrived at the new destination».

5.1 Remedies for lack of conformity

5.10 Introduction.

In the previous paragraph of this book, 5.0, we discussed lack of conformity according to the CISG and in what situations the buyer may claim lack of conformity. We will now assume that there exists a lack (or several) of conformity. This means that the seller has committed a breach of contract. We will now ask what remedies are available to the buyer for such breach of contract by the seller. The buyer may, according to the CISG articles of remedies (articles 46 to 52 and 74 to 77), claim remedies. See the overview in article 45 (1):

«If the seller fails to perform any of his obligations under the contract or this Convention, the buyer may:
(a) exercise the rights provided in articles 46 to 52;
(b) claim damages as provided in articles 74 to 77».

For the buyer to be able to raise any claim at all, it is *a basic condition that a lack of conformity exists*. If there is no lack of conformity, there is no way the buyer may claim remedies. In a conformity case we first have to decide if lack of conformity really exists. If the answer to that question is yes, we can go on to decide on remedies. Which remedy/remedies the buyer may claim, is to be decided depending on the circumstances in each particular case. It is mandatory that a lack of conformity exists, but that is not always sufficient. Each particular remedy requires additional conditions to be fulfilled for the buyer to be able to claim the remedy. We will now turn our attention to these additional conditions.

CISG article 45 applies if *the seller* «fails to perform his obligations». Such failure could also have been *caused by the buyer*, see article 80:

«A party may not rely on a failure of the other party to perform, to the extent that such failure was caused by the first party's act or omission».

We have to remember that the buyer, too, has obligations to fulfil in order to achieve delivery, see article 60:

«The buyer's obligation to take delivery consists:
(a) in doing all the acts which could reasonably be expected of him in order to enable the seller to make delivery; and
(b) in taking over the goods».

If the buyer has made – or has hired other people to make – drawings or technical specifications and these contain fatal errors we will have a breach of contract *by the buyer*. Similarly if the buyer has required the seller to hire a certain supplier or contract assistant, and one of these makes a mistake which influences the delivered goods.

5.11 Remedy of lack of conformity (by repair or by substitute goods).

5.110 Introduction. The buyer's right to such remedy is stated in CISG article 46 (2) and (3), while the seller's right to remedy is stated in article 48 (1). Here we must stress the two sides of this remedy question:

First: *The buyer* has a right to require remedy of the lack of conformity. This means that the seller has an obligation to act accordingly, even if the seller would prefer to compensate the lack of conformity in a different manner, for instance by a price reduction according to article 50. When the seller is situated in a foreign country, it may be complicated to obtain performance even if the buyer is entitled to require remedy, see article 28.

Second: *The seller,* on the other hand, has a right to remedy the lack of conformity. This means that the buyer has to accept such remedying even if he would prefer to have the lack of conformity compensated by a price reduction or to declare the contract avoided.

If the seller and the buyer are able to agree on how the lack of conformity is to be compensated, there is no problem, see article 29. But if they do not, the CISG gives either party the right to demand remedy of the lack of conformity, see articles 46 (2) and (3) and 48 (1) respectively.

Let us first discuss the cases where the buyer wants to have the faults remedied by repair or substitute goods. The buyer may require repair according to article 46 (3). Article 46 (2) decides on delivery of substitute goods.

5.111 The buyer requires performance according to the contract.

«If the goods do not conform with the contract», the CISG article 46 (3) gives the buyer the right to «require the seller to remedy the lack of conformity by repair».

If the repair imposes expenses on *the buyer*, he may claim damages according to articles 74 and 79.

Repair may, however, cause the seller substantial expenses. Article 46 (3) therefore includes a reservation; «unless this is unreasonable having regard to all the circumstances». In case of the latter the seller may refuse to repair the goods. Repair may, for instance, be very complicated to achieve, or it may be unreasonably expensive.

Besides unreasonable costs, the repair may cause the seller unreasonable inconvenience. The seller may, for instance, lack the skill and expertise needed to achieve a successful repair. In such cases the buyer may not want the seller to interfere with the goods either. The buyer may hire a third person to do the repair, and claim damage compensation according to articles 74 and 79, if not another alternative is more reasonable.

The buyer may claim repair even if the problem with the goods does not amount to a fundamental breach. If the goods are only slightly damaged, however, we cannot expect the seller to undertake disproportionate costs to repair it. Similarly if the goods are cheap: If for instance a cheap watch is faulty, it may be best for both parties if the seller delivers a substitute product or declares the contract avoided and gets his money back. In such cases the seller may prefer to deliver a substitute watch instead of trying to repair the defected one. On the other hand, in some cases small faults may be repaired by simple and cheap means.

CISG article 46 (2) gives the buyer a right to «require delivery of substitute goods only if the lack of conformity constitutes a fundamental breach of contract». This reminds us of article 49 on avoidance, which also requires fundamental breach. If the lack of conformity is *not* fundamental, however, the buyer may not choose between repair and substitute goods. He may then only claim repair according to article 46 (3), or reduce the price according to article 50.

By delivery of substitute goods the buyer receives a new product at the same time as he returns the goods that were delivered in the first place, see article 81 (2): «If both parties are bound to make restitution, they must do so concurrently». If the buyer is not able to return the goods, he loses the right to require substitute goods, according to article 82 (1). Remember the exceptions made in article 82 (2), though.

When the buyer requires remedying of the lack of conformity according to articles 46 (2) and (3), he has to require this «either in conjunction with notice given under article 39 or within a reasonable time thereafter». As we see, there are two notifications the buyer must give the seller; one general according to article 39 and then within a reasonable time thereafter, one requiring remedy according to article 46 (2)/(3). If the buyer has made up his mind about what to claim, he may combine these two notifications in one single «article 39-

notification». If the buyer fails to observe the notification paragraphs in due time, he loses the right to these remedies. The buyer may still claim price reduction and damages, but he cannot declare the contract avoided. This is because the CISG has a similar notification rule in article 49 (2).

The seller, too, must act in a timely manner. CISG article 47 (1) entitles *the buyer* to «fix an additional period of time of reasonable length for performance by the seller of his obligations». Again we deal with the word «reasonable» (as in article 46 (2) and (3)), and again its interpretation depends on the circumstances of each particular case.

If the seller manages to repair or supply substitute goods in time, article 47 (2) declares that

«The buyer may not, during that period, resort to any remedy for breach of contract. However, the buyer is not deprived thereby of any right he may have to claim damages for delay in performance».

During the additional period, which the buyer according to article 47 (2) has granted the seller, he is *not* allowed to change his mind and declare the contract avoided or claim price reduction. The buyer might have had a choice at first, but now that he has required repair or substitute goods within an additional period of time, he has made his choice and has to wait and see how well the seller uses his new chance to repair or substitute the goods. Only if the seller once again fails to perform according to the contract – he is too late or the goods still do not conform – the buyer may resort to other remedies.

Even if the seller eventually succeeds, the buyer may still have endured losses caused by the seller's delay in delivering conforming goods. In this case the buyer may claim damages according to articles 45 (1) letter b), 74 and 79. See also article 45 (2):

«The buyer is not deprived of any right he may have to claim damages by exercising his right to other remedies».

5.112 The seller's right to remedy lack of conformity.

Article § 48 attends to the remedy question seen from the seller's point of view:

«(1) Subject to article 49, the seller may, even after the date for delivery, remedy at his own expense any failure to perform his obligations, if he can do so without unreasonable delay and without causing the buyer unreasonable inconvenience or uncertainty of reimbursement by the seller of expenses advanced by the buyer. However, the buyer retains any right to claim damages as provided for in this Convention».

According to this article, the seller may try to meet the buyer's claims by offering to remedy his own breach of contract and eventually bring about a performance that conforms to the contract. This means repairing the goods or delivering substitute goods. If the seller succeeds in doing this, the buyer may lose his right to claim price reduction or cancel the contract. As to the latter we must bear in mind the opening phrase of article 48 (1): «Subject to article 49». This phrase was much disputed in the negotiations during the formation of the CISG convention and represents a compromise. Its meaning is most likely that the buyer is entitled to declare the contract avoided according to article 49 if the seller's breach of contract, despite an eventual successful remedying, still amounts to a fundamental breach. This is the case if the breaches of contract by the seller influence the buyer's total situation so severely that the criteria in article 25 are met. In other words the inconvenience and delay caused by the seller's breach of contract hits the buyer so hard that it would be reasonable to allow him to declare the contract avoided even if the seller eventually manages to bring about an acceptable performance.

In these considerations it is important to evaluate how well the seller meets the criteria in article 48 (1):

These three conditions must be met;

1) «Without unreasonable delay»,

2) Without «unreasonable inconvenience» for the buyer, and

3) Without «uncertainty of reimbursement by the seller of expenses advanced by the buyer».

Conditions 1 and 2 mainly require a consideration of the term «unreasonable»: What is an «unreasonable delay»? What is an «unreasonable inconvenience»? These questions must be answered based on a consideration of the circumstances in each particular case.

These two conditions are also interfering with each other: If a long period of time elapses before a remedy is provided by the seller, it will be much easier for the buyer to claim that he has suffered an unreasonable inconvenience. The buyer's problems may be so serious that the conditions in article 25 are met, giving him the right to declare the contract avoided according to article 49. An important part of this consideration is how badly the buyer's interests are hurt. Unreasonable inconvenience for the buyer will easily be the case if the seller's breach of contract leads to a hold in the buyer's business, even if the seller paying damages may cover the buyer's loss.

And the other way around; Substantial inconvenience coupled with short delay: Even if the lack of conformity is severe, as long as the seller supplies quick expert help and rapidly manages to address the severe problems successfully, the remedying may be accepted.

Condition 3 above says that the buyer is not obliged to accept the seller's remedying offer if the buyer has to pay for expenses in advance, for transport of the goods for instance, *and* the circumstances indicates that the seller will not be willing or able to reimburse the buyer with these expenses.

According to article 48 (2) the seller may request «the buyer to make known whether he will accept performance». The seller should in his request make sure that he includes *an indication of time* within which he will perform, as also indicated in article 48 (3). The buyer should not ignore this request, because if «the buyer does not comply with the request within a reasonable time, the seller may perform within the time indicated in his own request. The buyer may not, during that period of time, resort to any remedy which is inconsistent with performance by the seller.»

Even *after* this period of time it would still be impossible to claim such remedies. Even if the seller eventually, but too late, succeeds in performing according to the contract, inconsistent remedies will remain inconsistent. Such remedies are price reduction according to article 50 together with avoidance according to article 49. To claim damages, however, is not inconsistent, which is clearly stated in article 45 (2):

«The buyer is not deprived of any right he may have to claim damages by exercising his right to other remedies».

If the seller fails to perform accordingly within his own self indicated time, the buyer may now also resort to the remedies mentioned above: He can claim price reduction or, if the breach of contract has by now become fundamental, he can declare the contract avoided.

Article 48 (4), as well as article 47 (2), states that the notification must have reached the buyer in order to be effective. This is contrary to the general provision of article 27 about the transmission of notices.

5.113 The buyer's obligation to accept the seller's remedying of the lack of conformity.

It would be impossible for the seller to remedy a lack of conformity by repair if the buyer refuses to accept it. If the seller's remedying offer is in accordance with article 48 the buyer has no right to refuse it. If he still does, he loses his right to claim price reduction according to article 50. His claims for damages or avoidance will also be more likely to fail: It could be hard for the buyer to claim fundamental breach according to article 49 because the remedy which he has refused to accept could have improved the situation so that the definition of fundamental breach in article 25 is no longer met. According to article 77, a party must «take such measures as are reasonable in the circumstances to mitigate the loss», in order to claim damages. To permit the seller to remedy if the seller's offer is in accordance with article 49 is indeed a highly reasonable measure. Even if the buyer would rather make different claims, he has to accept that the seller uses his right to remedy the lack of conformity.

5.12 Price reduction.

A price reduction offers the buyer a compensation for having received less value than he should in accordance with the contract. The lack of conformity may reduce the value of the goods. The seller could also have delivered a smaller quantity than prescribed by the contract. In both these cases the best-balanced contract can be achieved by allowing the buyer a proportionally reduced price. The ancient Roman lawyers called this *actio quanti minoris.*

According to CISG article 50, the buyer may reduce the price. In some cases the buyer prefers to reduce the price instead of claiming remedying according to article 46 (2) or (3). The goods may still function satisfactorily even with the fault, as the case would be with an aesthetic flaw. The buyer might not always find it necessary or worthwhile to correct the fault.

Perhaps the buyer doubts the seller's ability to remedy effectively. The buyer then receives price reduction as a compensation for accepting goods that do not conform to the contract. Thus the buyer is not forced to spend money on repairing the goods, but can spend it any way he wants.

If the seller, according to article 48, offers to remedy his failure to perform according to the contract and actually succeeds in this, the buyer loses his right to reduce the price, see the second sentence of article 50.

Price reduction as a remedy is quite simple to manage. Both here and elsewhere in this chapter the basic condition is that a lack of conformity exits. But this lack of conformity does not have to be fundamental. Therefore it is easier to allow the buyer to reduce the contract price than to declare the contract avoided. According to article 49, avoidance requires fundamental breach.

Article 50 describes how the price reduction is to be calculated. The price reduction is equivalent to the reduced value. The lack of conformity must have actually led to this reduced value. If this is not the case, there will be no price reduction. This is of interest because not every lack of conformity leads to reduced value compared to the value of goods that do conform to the contract. If for instance the goods came in the wrong colour or design, or even the wrong size, this lack of conformity does not necessarily reduce the value of the goods. Therefore the buyer cannot demand a reduced price. If the breach is considered fundamental he may, however, require delivery of substitute goods (article 46) or declare the contract avoided (article 49).

If the lack of conformity does actually reduce the value of the goods, we must find out *how much* it has reduced the value. According to article 50 it is the value «at *the time for delivery*» that is decisive, and *not* the value at the time of contract formation or at the time when the lack of conformity was discovered. This is important to keep in mind if the goods undergo value fluctuations. The amount by which the price is to be reduced is stated in article 50: The buyer «may reduce the price in the same proportion as the value that the goods actually delivered had at the time of the delivery bears to the value that conforming goods would have had at that time». This means that the contract price shall be reduced in the same proportion as the lack of conformity reduces the value of the goods.

Example: The goods' value is 10 000, but a lack of conformity reduces their value by 1 000, i.e. 10 per cent. Then the contract price should also be reduced by 10 per cent. If the contract price is lower, for instance 8 000, the price reduction will be lower as well, only 800. On the other hand, if the contract price is higher, for instance 12 000, the price reduction will be relatively high, 1 200.

The text in article 50 defines the equation to be used: Reduced price divided by contract price equals the value of the non conforming goods delivered divided by the value of conforming goods.

$$\frac{\text{Reduced price}}{\text{Contract price}} = \frac{\text{Value delivered goods}}{\text{Value conforming goods}}$$

It may also be calculated this way: To find the reduced price we divide the value of the delivered goods by the value of conforming goods of the same type. Then we multiply the quotient by the contract price.

$$\text{Reduced price} = \frac{\text{Value delivered goods}}{\text{Value conforming goods}} * \text{contract price}$$

If the buyer was lucky during the previous price negotiations, he receives a relatively small price reduction when a fault is discovered. The buyer may then prefer to claim damages, for instance expenses for repair. On some occasions the buyer may claim both price reduction and damages. This could be the case if the buyer has had expenses, which are not covered by the price reduction. Damages will only cover expenses *not* covered by the price reduction; because the buyer should not be permitted to benefit from the seller's breach of contract. A price reduction is to be deducted if damage compensation is paid for the same expense.

Sometimes the price reduction is stipulated to equal the repair costs, but this is only when the repair costs equals the reduced value caused by the lack of conformity. On other occasions the repair costs can only be a factor in estimating the reduced value and thereby the price reduction. Such value estimations are often difficult to make.

5.13 The buyer declares the contract avoided.

5.130 Introduction

According to article 49, avoidance of the contract means that the sale is cancelled and the performance of the parties' obligations is discontinued. As a result the parties may claim restitution of whatever they have supplied or paid under the contract, see article 81 (2). The non-conforming goods must be returned to the seller while at the same time the seller must return money paid by the buyer under the contract, concurrently as article 81 (2) 2nd sentence requires.

In addition it is possible for the buyer to claim damage compensation. Price reduction or remedying by repair or by substitute goods, however, may not be claimed now. Since the claims mentioned assume that the contract is not cancelled, they are inconsistent with avoidance. It is up to the buyer to choose whether to take advantage of article 49 and declare the contract avoided, or to remedy the consequences of the lack of conformity otherwise. The seller cannot influence the buyer's choice, unless he succeeds in remedying according to article 48.

5.131 Fundamental breach.

Breach of contract is not sufficient to declare a contract avoided. According to article 49 and principles of the general law of contract, the breach has to be fundamental. This condition resembles article 46 (2) concerning request for delivery of substitute goods. We have to consider how severely the lack of conformity influences the buyer and his business, see article 25:

«A breach of contract committed by one of the parties is fundamental if it results in such detriment to the other party as substantially to deprive him of what he is entitled to expect under the contract, unless the party in breach did not foresee and a reasonable person of the same kind in the same circumstances would not have foreseen such a result».

We have already seen (part 5.0 of this book) that it is often a difficult task to decide if a lack of conformity exists. It is also difficult to decide whether the lack of conformity is fundamental or not. A lot of the same factors are relevant both in the conformity decision as well as in the fundamental breach decision: We must compare the goods the seller has actually delivered, with goods conforming to the contract. *What actually caused* the lack of conformity is irrelevant. But if the lack of conformity is in fact caused by negligence on the seller's side or worse even; by plain carelessness or deliberate violation of the obligations in the contract, such circumstances will count in the direction of fundamental breach.

We have to bear in mind that avoidance is a remedy, which is likely to hit the seller very hard. Therefore our consideration must include whether or not the buyer's problems can be satisfactorily solved by other remedies; for instance by asking if the seller is willing to and capable of remedying the lack of conformity by repair, by delivery of substitution goods, or by paying price reduction or damage compensation. A breach of contract is not fundamental if the buyer's needs are satisfactorily taken care of by alternative remedies. The seller may not, for instance, be able to repair the goods himself, but the goods can easily and sufficiently be repaired by hired experts. If the seller pays for the expenses suffered by the buyer from the breach, there may be no fundamental breach left.

Time is also an important factor for the decision on fundamental breach. According to article 48 (1), the seller has to remedy «without unreasonable delay» if the buyer is to be bound to accept the seller's remedying. Whether the seller succeeds or not will influence the decision. We must consider how substantial the lack of conformity is, how much time has elapsed and what inconvenience the buyer has experienced. The question is whether or not the total of non-conformity amounts to fundamental breach of contract. A combination of delayed delivery and lack of conformity takes place when flawed goods are delivered too late. We can ask if the buyer's situation in total is so severe that he should reasonably be entitled to claim that the conditions in article 25 are met: Is it fair to grant him the right to cancel the contract?

5.132. Notification.

When the buyer wants to declare the contract avoided, he must not fail to observe his obligation according to article 49 (2) letter b) to let the seller know. The buyer must notify the seller within a reasonable time «after he knew or ought to have known of the breach». This is called a specified notice, because the seller has to be informed that the buyer declares the contract avoided.

According to article 39 (1), it is sufficient for the buyer simply to specify the nature of the lack of conformity. This notice must be given «within a reasonable time», and according to article 49 (2), letter b) it has to be followed by another message also «within a reasonable time» where the buyer declares the contract avoided.

What «reasonable time» actually means, depends on the circumstances in each particular case. The notification according to article 39 (1) and the notification according to article 49 (2) letter b) do not need to be sent at the same time, but the buyer *may still choose* to do so. According to article 39 (2), a neutral notice ought to be given rapidly. At this point of time it is sufficient to specify the nature of the lack of conformity, for instance that the object does not function as expected, without any careful examination of the goods in order to decide how to deal with the lack of conformity. If the buyer because of these problems should want to declare the contract avoided, however, he must, according to article 49 (2) letter b), do so within a reasonable time.

The buyer cannot claim the contract avoided until he sees how the seller's attempt to remedy works out. A patient buyer might not declare the contract avoided until the seller has made several unsuccessful attempts to repair the goods. As long as the buyer does so within a reasonable time after he discovers or ought to have discovered that the last attempt also turned out to fail, he may still cancel the contract. We should not punish a buyer who is patient and gives the seller several attempts to remedy the lack of conformity. On the other hand the buyer should not wait too long before suggesting that avoidance may be the consequence. This prevents the seller from being misled to believe that the buyer eventually will be satisfied with price reduction or damage compensation.

It is a good idea for the buyer to fix an additional period of time according to article 47, and make this his final offer. If the seller still fails to repair the fault, the buyer has to confirm his choice to declare the contract avoided by notifying the seller according to article 49 (2) letter b) subparagraph (ii). Subparagraph (iii) in article 49 (2) letter b) states similarly if the period of time is indicated by *the seller* according to article 48 (2).

We must keep in mind that the buyer may need some time to decide if he wants to cancel the contract or not. On the other hand the seller needs to know the buyer's decision. It is a serious situation for the seller and he needs to act quickly to prevent severe losses. We will comment further on the term «reasonable time» in paragraph 7.21 later in this book.

5.14 The buyer claims damages.

Much like the preceding remedies damage compensation also requires that *breach of contract* by lack of conformity exists. This is stated in article 45 (1) as well as articles 74 and 79.

According to article 74 damages «consist of a sum equal to the loss, including loss of profit, suffered by the other party as a consequence of the breach». The buyer may claim other remedies in addition to damages, see article 45 (2). Damages may be combined with other remedies following the breach of contract: For instance declaring the contract avoided may be followed by a claim for damages covering the increased expenses suffered when ordering the same type of goods from a different supplier who charges a higher price (see article 75). In the same way the buyer may have suffered losses due to the breach of contract even if the seller eventually succeeds in remedying the lack of conformity. That the fault has now been remedied by repair does not prevent the buyer from claiming damages for costs already suffered.

However, CISG article 79 exempts the seller from liability if he proves that the lack of conformity «was due to an impediment beyond his control and that he could not reasonably be expected to have taken the impediment into account at the time of the conclusion of the contract or to have avoided or overcome it or its consequences». If the breach of contract is due to this type of impediment the seller is exempt from the buyer's damages claim. But on the other hand the seller must accept that the buyer raises other claims instead, such as price reduction, remedying or even avoidance, see article 79 (5): «Nothing in this article prevents either party from exercising any right other than to claim damages under this Convention».

Earlier (paragraph 4.121 of this book) we discussed the conditions for the seller's exemption from liability for damages due to impediments causing delayed (or no) delivery. The considerations are the same when the breach of contract is lack of conformity. However, it is still reasonable to make some comments on the application of these articles on breach of contract by lack of conformity. We should stress that all four conditions of article 79 (1) have to be met for the seller to be exempt from liability.
The seller has to pay damages unless these four conditions are met according to article 79:

1) The lack of conformity must be due to an impediment
2) This impediment must lie beyond the seller's control
3) The seller could not reasonably be expected to have taken the impediment into account at the time of the conclusion of the contract
4) The seller could not reasonably be expected to have avoided or overcome the impediment or its consequences.

One fault in itself will not be an exempting impediment even if this fault was hidden and impossible for a throughout careful seller or the seller's people to detect or overcome the consequences of. We must ask whether the fault is due to an impediment that meets the exemption conditions and whether this impediment constitutes an impediment for conforming delivery.

If this is not the case, the seller must pay damage compensation, if not the same fault has destroyed all species of these particular goods. An example of the latter is if the contract requires delivery of 10 tons of potatoes from a certain farm and this farm's whole crop is damaged by frost. This leads to the seller's exemption from his obligation to pay damages. If the contract had simply said potatoes of a certain type, the result would have been different.

When the contract concerns delivery of a particular object, which is unique and cannot be substituted with another object, it might be reasonable to admit the seller a possibility of exemption. This is because here the seller has no chance of finding any alternative goods to deliver. But exemption is not granted, because article 79 (1) points out a strict causation criterion: «The failure was due to an impediment». Thereby the cause of the fault has to be beyond the seller's control and thus making him unable to deliver conforming goods. Even if the seller could not possibly deliver another object, he would often have been able to repair the goods and then deliver. Repair is not possible, however, if the fault is hidden. The hidden fault is an impediment for repair, but the question in article 79 (1) is if the fault itself is caused by an impediment. That is not the exact same question. Therefore the buyer may claim damages even if the lack of conformity is due to a hidden fault.

An example: A used machine has been sold. A part in the motor turned out to be defected. This part could have been substituted and spare parts were available. It was not substituted, however, because the defect was hidden and not possible to discover by normal testing. Here damage compensation has to be paid (provided the other conditions for damages are met and there are actually losses to be paid for). As long as it was technically possible to substitute the faulty particle, it is irrelevant if this was not done because the fault could not be discovered. Since the sold product was a used machine, however, we must stress that breach of contract must exist, which often is *not* the case when things are sold second-hand and as is.

The interpretation of article 79 (1) above may not be undisputed. The word impediment also seems to cover hidden faults. A hidden fault is seen as an impediment making delivery of conforming goods impossible. This may be reasonable considering the fact that the seller had no real possibility to act otherwise, since the fault could not have been discovered even with a fully careful examination and testing of the thing.

5.141 Lack of conformity due to a third person.

We will now discuss the seller's liability for lack of conformity that is due to the failure of a third person whom the seller has engaged to perform the whole or a part of the contract, see article 79 (2). This article also applies to delays caused by a third person (se paragraph 4.122 earlier in this book). The seller is obviously liable for mistakes done by his own employees because he can easily instruct them. Generally in the law of contract the seller is also liable for negligence due to third persons he cannot instruct. CISG article 79 (2) with its so-called «double force majeure» strikes the seller even harder:

«If the party's failure is due to the failure by a third person whom he has engaged to perform the whole or a part of the contract, that party is exempt from liability only if: (a) he is exempt under the preceding paragraph; and (b) the person whom he has so engaged would be so exempt if the provisions of that paragraph were applied to him».

Even if the seller or a third person engaged by him is not to blame for negligence, the seller may still be liable according to this article. The seller is only exempt from liability if *both* the seller *and* the third person engaged by him are struck by a liability-exempting impediment. See further details on article 79 in paragraph 4.122 earlier in this book.

5.2 Third party claims

In some cases a third party tries to intervene in the contract between the seller and the buyer. This third party may claim that he owns the goods and that the seller thus has no right to sell it to the buyer (CISG article 41). Furthermore the third party may claim to have rights concerning the goods, for instance industrial property/intellectual property rights (article 42).

Article 41: «The seller must deliver goods which are free from any right or claim of a third party, unless the buyer agreed to take the goods subject to that right or claim».

We see here that a mere *claim* is sufficient. The buyer shall not be forced into a lawsuit in order to obtain full rights of the goods. The buyer may accept to buy the goods despite of the claim. It could be important for the buyer to have the goods, and it may be obvious that the claim is unfounded. This is often a question of price; the buyer is willing to risk legal trouble if the price is reduced accordingly.

Here, as elsewhere in the law of contract the interpretation of the parties' contract, their conduct and the surrounding circumstances are important.

Depending on the law of the State the third party may lose his right when the goods are sold to a careful buyer in good faith. Even so the buyer may choose to respect the third person's right when he becomes aware of it. A buyer will generally find it morally uncomfortable to be in possession of goods belonging to a third person or to which a third party has rights. The seller is then liable according to article 41, and the buyer may claim remedies for breach of contract by the seller.

If the third party's claim is based on industrial/intellectual property article 42 applies instead:

«(1) The seller must deliver goods which are free from any right or claim of a third party based on industrial property or other intellectual property, of which at the time of the conclusion of the contract the seller knew or could not have been unaware, provided that the right or claim is based on industrial property or other intellectual property:
(a) under the law of the State where the goods will be resold or otherwise used, if it was contemplated by the parties at the time

of the conclusion of the contract that the goods would be resold or otherwise used in that State; or
(b) in any other case, under the law of the State where the buyer has his place of business.»

If the buyer is to blame, article 42 (2) makes an exception:
«The obligation of the seller under the preceding paragraph does not extend to cases where:
(a) at the time of the conclusion of the contract the buyer knew or could not have been unaware of the right or claim; or
(b) the right or claim results from the seller's compliance with technical drawings, designs, formulae or other such specifications furnished by the buyer».

If a buyer finds himself in the situation described in either article 41 or article 42, he has to notify the seller according to article 43. If he does not do so the buyer loses his right to claim remedies according to CISG section III. Nevertheless according to article 44 the buyer is entitled to some claims if he had a «reasonable excuse for his failure to give the required notice».

If the seller «knew of the right or claim of the third party and the nature of it», he has no reasonable right to expect a notice, see article 43 (2). No contract party has the right to be informed of what he already knows. Similar articles usually add the words «ought to have known», but this is not the case here.

According to articles 41 and 42 lack of conformity gives the buyer, in the same way as other kinds of breach of contract by the seller, remedies according to CISG Section III. The buyer may require remedying of the fault or claim a price reduction. If the lack of conformity amounts to a fundamental breach, the buyer may declare the contract avoided. This is the case if the seller has sold goods, which he did not own in the first place. The buyer may also claim damage compensation according to articles 74 to 79.

Here, as elsewhere, it is not a general condition that the seller is to blame for the situation. The seller is liable even if he had good reasons to believe that he had full and undisputed rights to the goods. This lack of conformity does not necessarily mean that the seller is guilty of negligence or carelessness.

Chapter 6. Obligations of the buyer

6.1 Introduction. Delayed or no payment. The buyer's obligation to take delivery.

In this chapter the buyer is the one who has failed to perform according to the contract. This is contrary to the previous chapters (chapters 4 and 5) about breach of contract by the seller. The latter raises a host of questions because a seller is able to breach the contract in many respects. Breach of contract by the buyer, on the other hand, is by far simpler: Transferring a sum of money and receiving the goods are relatively uncomplicated tasks to undertake:

The buyer's principal obligation is to pay the price in time. To decide on breach of contract is then a quite simple question.

The principal rule concerning the buyer's breach of contract is found in article 61:

« (1) If the buyer fails to perform any of his obligations under the contract or this Convention, the seller may:
(a) exercise the rights provided in articles 62 to 65;
(b) claim damages as provided in articles 74 to 77.
(2) The seller is not deprived of any right he may have to claim damages by exercising his right to other remedies.
(3) No period of grace may be granted to the buyer by a court or arbitral tribunal when the seller resorts to a remedy for breach of contract».

Also note article 80, according to which a party *may not* «rely on a failure of the other party to perform, to the extent that such failure was caused by the first party's act or omission». Therefore we must first find out if the buyer's breach of contract is due to the seller; for instance if the seller has not delivered according to the contract. Also see article 58 about payment on delivery.

6.2 Remedies for breach of contract by the buyer.

6.20 The seller requires the buyer to perform his obligations.

6.200 Introduction. If the buyer does not pay in time, the seller may require him to pay the price, see article 62. The buyer's obligation to pay the price follows from the contract and for the seller to cash it in is not really a remedy for *breach* of the contract. When the buyer's payment is due, but still unpaid, the seller will have to undertake efforts to enforce payment. This often represents a lot of inconvenience for the seller, including trying to get access to the legal system in the home state of the buyer. If the buyer eventually is found to be completely without funds, the process may in addition prove costly for the seller.

6.201 Interest.

If the buyer does not pay in time, he will have to pay interest according to article 78. The CISG does not, however, state any interest rate. During the negotiations preceding the formation of the convention, no agreement was reached beyond the short sentence of article 78. We must bear in mind that the CISG has member states from all over the globe, and thus of different cultural, religious and political views. This is truly one of the convention's strengths, but on certain issues, like this concerning interest, it forces the convention to be silent. The interest question will therefore depend on the law of the countries involved. If both the seller's and the buyer's countries have interest rates at about the same level, the buyer should have to pay this rate. But if the law of the parties' states prohibits interest, it may in fact be impossible for the seller to have his interest claim recognised by the legal system.

6.21 The seller declares the contract avoided

6.210 Fundamental breach.

The seller is entitled to declare the contract avoided according to article 64 letter a) if «the failure by the buyer to perform any of his obligations under the contract or this Convention amounts to a fundamental breach of contract».

It is up to the seller to decide whether he will take advantage of this right or not, even if the delay in payment amounts to fundamental breach. In some cases the seller may prefer to stick to the contract; provided he evaluates the buyer to be able to pay.

How much delay is needed for the delay to amount to a fundamental breach? Here the buyer is the one who has failed to perform according to the contract, but the considerations will be the same as in article 49 where the seller fails to deliver the goods in time (see chapter 4 of this book). In both cases article 25 applies. We must consider how much the delay affects the seller and his business, and not whether the buyer is to blame for the situation or not. We must also look at what type of contract it is and see if we are dealing with a business where correct payment is essential, for instance if the goods are undergoing rapid price fluctuations. One party should not be allowed to speculate at the other party's expense.

Of course, it is also of importance whether the whole contract sum is unpaid or if just a minor part of the price remains to be settled.

If the price *is paid*, however, even if it is too late, article 64 (2) applies:

«However, in cases where the buyer has paid the price, the seller loses the right to declare the contract avoided unless he does so:

(a) in respect of late performance by the buyer, before the seller has become aware that performance has been rendered».

6.211 Additional period of time.

According to the CISG article 63 the seller «may fix an additional period of time of reasonable length for performance by the buyer of his obligations». This article is to be read in connection with article 64 (2) letter b) which allows the seller to declare the contract avoided if the buyer still does not pay.

Article 63 is a parallel to article 47 concerning delay on the part of the seller, and is to be interpreted in the same way (see paragraph 4.112 earlier in this book).

6.22 The seller claims damages.

If the seller has suffered expenses due to the buyer's breach of contract, the seller may claim damage compensation according to CISG articles 74 to 79.

Damage compensation will be of particular interest if the seller has to declare the contract avoided. The seller has still got the goods and will have to dispose of them in the best way possible, which may not, at this time, be an easy task. When the seller is now forced to try to sell the goods to another customer, he may not be able to get a favourable price. The seller may then take advantage of article 75 and claim damages from the buyer: The seller may «recover the difference between the contract price and the price in the substitute transaction as well as further damages recoverable under article 74».

If the seller does not declare the contract avoided, but sticks to the contract and demands payment, he may still suffer expenses, for instance in order to force the buyer to pay or due to currency fluctuations. The buyer is liable according to article 74, no matter what has caused the delayed payment. Even if the buyer is not to blame for his financial problems, which for instance could have been caused by delayed payment from the buyer's own debtors, the buyer is still liable according to this article. The buyer is exempt only if he meets all the conditions in article 79 (1): The buyer must prove that his failure to pay «was due to an impediment beyond his control and that he could not reasonably be expected to have taken the impediment into account at the time of the conclusion of the contract or to have avoided or overcome its consequences».

6.3 The buyer's obligation to take delivery.

The principal obligation of the buyer under a sales contract is to pay the price. But the buyer also has an obligation according to article 53 to take delivery and according to article 54 to take steps necessary to ensure that the seller receives correct payment. On many occasions the contract requires the buyer to «specify the form, measurement or other features of the goods», see article 65. Such specifications are necessary in most contracts for the supply of goods to be manufactured or produced.

It may seem needless to state that the buyer has to take delivery. For the buyer it is important to be able to receive the goods, otherwise he would not have bought them in the first place. There are occasions, however, when the seller is not necessarily satisfied even if he has received payment for the goods. When the seller has sold used machinery or goods from a warehouse that he now intends to use for other purposes, or when he has sold poisonous waste materials, it is vital for him that the buyer actually takes over the goods. On such occasions it is very important for the seller to have the goods transported away.

CISG article 64 entitles the seller to declare the contract avoided «if the failure by the buyer to perform any of his obligations under the contract or this Convention amounts to a fundamental breach of contract». As elsewhere in the law of contract a fundamental breach is necessary to declare a contract avoided. The seller may cancel the contract only if the failing performance as a whole is considered a fundamental breach. For instance, he has to reduce his production because the goods ordered by the buyer are taking up considerable space in the seller's warehouse. The seller's problems have to be quite serious to allow him to declare the contract avoided because the buyer does not take over the goods in time. In most cases the failure to take over the goods will be combined with failure to pay the price. This combination may amount to fundamental breach. In such cases the buyer will, according to article 85, have to reimburse the seller's reasonable expenses to preserve the goods.

If the seller has suffered other losses due to the buyer's failure to take over the goods, he may, depending on the circumstances, be entitled to claim damages according to articles 74 to 80.

Chapter 7 Common provisions

7.0 Introduction

Having in the three previous chapters (chapters 4 to 6) discussed different kinds of breach of contract we will now focus on some *general questions*, which apply to all kinds of breach of contract. Thereby we might bring together some loose ends from the previous chapters.

7.1 Damages

7.10 Principal conditions for claiming damages.

We will now attend to the stipulation of damages when a party is entitled to damages due to a breach of contract by the other contract party. For a party to claim damages some principal conditions have to be met. First there has to be a legal basis for the claim. In the CISG we find legal basis in article 45 (1) letter b) concerning damages if the seller fails to perform according to the contract and article 61 (1) letter b) concerning damages if the buyer fails to do so: Also see the preceding chapters 4 to 6 of this book.

Another principal condition that has to be met is economic loss: The contract party claiming damages must be able to prove that he has suffered loss, including loss of profit, as a consequence of the breach of contract, see article 74: The loss has to be economic, which means that it must be measured in money. If the loss cannot be measured in this way, it is not likely to be compensated, like for instance inconvenience and trouble caused by the other party's breach of contract.

On some occasions it is possible for the contract party subject to a breach of contract to actually profit from avoiding the contract because he had made a bad bargain in the first place. In that case there is no economic loss, and therefore no damages to be paid. We cannot stipulate the damages to a negative figure.

A third principal condition for damages is *adequate and foreseeable causation* from the breach of contract by one party and the economic loss suffered by the other party. We must be able to put the loss in connection with the breach of contract. Losses, which would have been suffered anyway, due to other causes, will not be compensated by the damages paid. In addition to proving a real connection, it is also required that the connection must be sufficiently close (adequate). The loss must be foreseeable. The mere fact that a party has committed breach of contract does not alone give the other party any reasonable right to hold him responsible for every distant and indirectly connected consequence of the actual breach of the contract. This is expressed in CISG article 74, 2nd sentence, stating:

«Such damages may not exceed the loss which the party in breach foresaw or ought to have foreseen at the time of the conclusion of the contract, in the light of the facts and matters of which he then knew or ought to have known, as a possible consequence of the breach of contract».

7.11 Price difference.

CISG articles 75 and 76 prescribe recovery of price difference. These articles concern damage compensation to cover the price difference in cases where one contract party declares the contract avoided: This contract party will then have to find a new and substitute contract party able to replace the current contract party, who fundamentally failed to perform according to the contract. We thus see that these articles apply to both parties; the buyer gets replacement goods from another seller or the seller resells the goods to another buyer. This will often make it difficult for them to get as good a bargain as they obtained in the first contract. Thereby they suffer loss.

If the buyer cancels the contract due to breach of contract by the seller, the buyer may, according to article 75, buy similar goods from another seller. If this turns out to be more expensive he may claim damage compensation to recover the price difference. If the seller is the one who declares the contract avoided, he may claim damages in the same way. The seller still possesses the goods, which he will now have to sell to another buyer. If this sale does not obtain the same price, the seller is entitled to claim the price difference from the buyer. Article 75 requires the substitute transaction to be undertaken «in a reasonable manner and within a reasonable time after avoidance».

Even if a substitute transaction is not undertaken, price difference may still be claimed. In this case a hypothetical price difference will be stipulated according to article 76. To find the price difference we compare the contract price of the contract that is now cancelled with «the current price at the time of avoidance».

The term «current price» is explained in article 76 (2):

«For the purposes of the preceding paragraph, the current price is the price prevailing at the place where delivery of the goods should have been made or, if there is no current price at that place, the price at such other place as serves as a reasonable substitute, making due allowance for differences in the cost of transporting the goods».

This current price, however, may be subject to fluctuations as time passes. Article 76 (1) gives two alternatives as to which time to apply in order to find the price difference. The decisive fact is whether the buyer *has already taken over the goods or not* at the time when he declares the contract avoided. If the buyer has actually taken over the goods at that time, we use the current price «at the time of such taking over» when finding the price difference, se article 76 (1), 2nd sentence. If he has *not* taken over the goods at that time, article 76 (1), 1st sentence applies, and «the current price at the time of avoidance» is to be used. In this case no time of taking over exists, and article 76 (2), 2nd sentence is rendered logic inapplicable.

The main purpose of article 76 (1) is to avoid speculations at the other contract party's expense. The party claiming damage compensation is taken care of by this party's right to rather choose to buy goods in replacement. Thereby, according to article 75, he may in the calculation use the price he actually paid. This way he will get the exact price difference covered.

7.12 A party's obligation to mitigate his losses.

According to CISG article 77 a «party who relies on a breach of contract must take such measures as are reasonable in the circumstances to mitigate the loss, including loss of profit, resulting from the breach».

This article is in accordance with a general principle of the law of contract and applies to both the seller's and the buyer's breach of contract.

The party, who has suffered loss due to a breach of contract by the other party, should obviously not be able to exploit the situation in order to obtain greater damage compensation than what is actually caused by the breach of contract. He should not just sit back and watch his losses increase day by day either, counting on the party in breach to pay for them. This is the case even if he does not directly profit from his inactivity and lack of initiative. Article 77 requires him to take some action, for instance by carefully performing a substitute transaction within a reasonable time.

If the party relying on a breach of contract does not do what he should according to article 77 he may lose his damages claim or have it reduced:

«If he fails to take such measures, the party in breach may claim a reduction in the damages in the amount by which the loss should have been mitigated» (article 77).

On the other hand, these considerations should not be based on *belated wisdom*. At the time when the breach of contract occurs the exact consequences may be difficult to estimate. The important factor is how the circumstances appeared to this party when he decided what to do or not to do. We must also grant him a reasonable period of time to consider his options before mitigation remedies are put into action.

7.2 Notification of breach of contract

7.20 Introduction.

If breach of contract by one of the contract parties occurs, the other party is supposed to take action. He can not just let things float, but has to let the party in breach know about the breach and the fact that it may lead to claims. This kind of action is often called notification, and is a vital part of the «observance of good faith in international trade», which is expressed in CISG article 7 (1).

Here are two types of articles the parties should be aware of:

1) Articles on notification immediately following the breach of contract, as soon as a contract party is – or should have been aware of – the breach of contract.

2) An ultimate period of time of two years according to article 39 (2) if the buyer will rely on lack of conformity with the contract.

7.21 Notification directly following the breach of contract.

Articles requiring notification following the breach of contract aim to give the contract party in breach a warning that the other party may raise claims due to the breach of contract. Thereby he has a chance to contradict the claim or try to remedy his breach of contract, for instance by repair. Both parties will usually benefit from the opportunity to handle the alleged breach of contract as soon as possible.

We will focus on situations where there has been performance, but this performance has not been according to the contract (delayed or not conforming).

If the goods do not conform with the contract, the CISG's articles about general notification apply, see articles 39 and 43. The reason behind these articles is the seller's need to know whether the goods he delivered are conforming with the contract or not. Such a general notification is not required if the goods are delivered too late or the price is paid too late. This is due to the fact that the party in breach in these cases is aware – or should be aware – of his own delay and that this may lead to claims from the other contract party. The party in breach does not need to be notified until claims are actually made. Nevertheless, the principles of «good faith in international trade» (see article 7 (1)) and loyalty should encourage the contract parties to keep each other mutually informed.

When it comes to cases of nonconforming goods, this is how the convention works: First the buyer gives «notice to the seller specifying the nature of the lack of conformity», see article 39 (1). Such notification is to be given «within a reasonable time». This means that the buyer must be given the time to inspect the goods and consider the lack of conformity. He cannot, however, take his time to consider what kind of claims he will raise or how he will handle the case. All the seller needs to know at this point is that a lack of conformity exists.

When this general notification has been made, the next step is for the buyer to consider whether or not he will declare the contract avoided because of the lack of conformity. If he decides to do so, the CISG article 49 (2) requires him to let the seller know: The buyer must give a specified notification «within a reasonable time». If the buyer prefers the lack of conformity to be remedied by substitute goods or by repair – he will also have to give the seller a specified notification, as requested by the regulations in article 46 (2) and (3).

For the claims just mentioned the CISG requires both a general notification and a specified notification on occasions of lack of conformity. However, on occasions of delayed delivery or delayed payment a general notification is sufficient, also for avoidance claims. But again we should remind of the principles in the contract law of «good faith in international trade» (see article 7 (1)) and loyalty, and their focus on communication between contract parties.

We have now seen that a buyer who declares the contract avoided or requires remedying by substitute goods or by repair, has to raise these claims within a reasonable time. If not he loses his right to these claims (i.e. he has to settle for other remedies for breach of contract which might be available to him). This is stated in article 49 (2) for delayed or nonconforming delivery and article 46 (2) and (3) for remedying.

Article 64 (2) applies to delayed payment. If the seller is aware that the payment has been made, he may not declare the contract avoided. When the price eventually is paid, even if it is too late, the seller's need for security should be satisfied. It will therefore be sufficient to claim interest according to article 78. See chapter 6 earlier in this book.

A specific notification is required when the contract is declared avoided. A cancellation of the contract is a very strong reaction, and it is extremely important for the party in breach to be informed whether the other party intends to make such a claim.

Also when remedying of faults is claimed, a specific notification has to be made, for much the same reasons, see article 46 (2) and (3). This specific notification, however, may according to these paragraphs be combined with the general lack of conformity notification that is required by article 39.

When articles 39 (1), 43 (1), 46 (2) and (3), 48 (2), 49 (2), 64 (2) and 73 (2) require notification «within a reasonable period of time», this is a term which has to be applied with consideration taken to all relevant circumstances in each particular case, as well as the principle of «good faith in international trade» (see article 7 (1)). How much time is reasonable depends on the goods and on who the contract parties are. When avoidance is an option, the party claiming cancellation may need some time to consider what his options are before he decides to take advantage of such a strong remedy as a cancellation.

Article 49 (2), letter a) states that the «reasonable period of time» starts when the buyer – who wants to cancel the contract because of late delivery – «has become aware that delivery has been made».

In article 49 (2) letter b), however, the «reasonable time» starts when the buyer «knew or ought to have known of the breach» of contract. This is because the buyer now wants to cancel the contract due to lack of conformity. If the goods suffer from faults that are difficult for the buyer to discover, some time may already have elapsed before the «reasonable time» starts to run.

It is also important to consider whether or not the buyer should have discovered the lack of conformity at an earlier point. In this case «reasonable time» starts at the moment he ought to have known of the breach of contract. For instance, if the buyer discovers fault in the goods in March and then notifies the seller, this notification may not be in time if the buyer ought to have discovered the fault back in October. The period from

October to March may fall beyond «a reasonable time». In the consideration of what the buyer ought to know or not we are likely to meet considerable problems as to evidence and proof. It is a very difficult task to decide the exact moment the lack of conformity ought to have been discovered.

Some of the most obvious and visible faults found in the goods are already excluded by article 35 (3): If the buyer already at the time of the conclusion of the contract «knew or could not have been unaware of such lack of conformity» the seller is not liable. This, however, only applies to severely negligent buyers. «Could not have been aware of» is a very strong term, even stronger than the term «ought to».

By using the term «ought to» article 38 (3) indicates that a negligent buyer is likely to lose his claims against the seller if the buyer does not discover faults, which he ought to have discovered on delivery of the goods. The buyer must examine the good as soon as possible in the transmission process, and not later than the time the goods have reached their final destination.

Article 38 does not go into detail about how the examination is to be undertaken. The normal business practice will be of interest, especially if both seller and buyer are familiar with it. It is reasonable to at least examine if the packages are damaged or not. In a delivery with many individual parcels we cannot expect the buyer to look through them all. However, it may be reasonable to pick some random parcels for further examination. If the goods are technically complicated machinery careful testing may be required.

According to article 38 the quality of the examination undertaken must be taken into consideration when we are to decide *when* article 39 expects the buyer to discover the lack of conformity. Furthermore a seller cannot blame the buyer for not doing his job according to articles 38 and 39 if the seller himself knew of or could not have been unaware of the lack of conformity. See article 40, which term «could not have been unaware of», however, requires – as mentioned above – a strong degree of negligence of the seller.

7.22 Notification within two years.

We have just seen that CISG article 39 (1) requires the buyer to «give notice to the seller specifying the nature of the lack of conformity within a reasonable time after he has discovered it or ought to have discovered it». According to article 39 (2), this notification has to be given «at the latest within a period of two years from the date on which the goods were actually handed over to the buyer».

Mark the term «*at the latest*». It does not matter if the faults are hidden and could not possibly have been discovered within this period of two years. After two years a seller is to consider the contract of sale to be settled. Another factor is that the *problems of proof* will grow bigger as time elapses. After several years the buyer will have a tough task trying to prove that the lack of conformity already existed when the goods were delivered, see articles 36 and 67 and chapter 5 earlier in this book. The consideration of such factors led the CISG to decide on a period of two years. Two years is a long time, which can easily cause problems when deciding if the fault existed at the time the goods were delivered.

According article 39 (2) the two-year period starts to run «the date on which the goods were actually handed over to the buyer». The crucial time is when the goods were actually received by the buyer, and not the more technical legal time for the passing of the risk or the time of delivery. This is reasonable since it is not until he receives the goods that the buyer has the full opportunity to discover possible hidden faults.

As we have seen above the seller cannot rely on article 39 if he has clearly been negligent, see article 40.

7.3 Return of the goods when the contract is avoided or substitute goods are delivered

7.30 Introduction.

We will now focus on how to deal with the situation where a contract is avoided or the buyer requires the seller to deliver substitute goods. On certain conditions the buyer as well as the seller may declare the contract avoided due to breach of contract by the other party. However, if the goods do not conform with the contract the buyer may, depending on the circumstances, require the seller to deliver substitute goods instead. The seller may choose to make an offer himself, or try to meet the buyer's claims by the delivery of substitute goods. The conditions having to be met in order to make such claims are described in chapters 4 – 6 above. We will now assume that these conditions are met.

«Avoidance of the contract releases both parties from their obligations under it, subject to any damages which may be due», is stated in article 81 (1). In other words the contract is still valid, which again means that damage compensation according to article 74 may be claimed in addition to avoidance, if the conditions for damages are met, see also article 79.

The easiest case scenario is when no party has performed anything at all under the now avoided contract. The parties are then, according to article 81 (1), simply released from their obligations to perform.

If one or both parties have fulfilled the contract, wholly or in part, a restitution of whatever the parties have supplied or paid, has to take place, see article 81 (2). This article also decides that if «both parties are bound to make restitution, they must do so concurrently».

7.31 Restitution substantially in the condition in which he received the goods, CISG chapter V.

Restitution *by the seller* does not raise many questions: He has to pay back the sum of money he received from the buyer. According to article 84 (1), the seller must also pay interest on it, starting from «the date on which the price was paid». The buyer, on the other hand, has to pay back the profit or benefit goods brought him while he possessed it; see article 84 (2) which requires the buyer to account «to the seller for all benefits which he has derived from the goods or part of them». The buyer has to account for the net profit. He may deduct costs and disadvantages, for instance such caused by having to use a defective thing.

Restitution by *the buyer* is more complicated in other respects as well. CISG article 81 (1) requires the buyer to «make restitution of the goods substantially in the condition in which he received them». If not he loses his «right to declare the contract avoided or to require the seller to deliver substitute goods».

Nevertheless, goods are bought to be used: When the buyer (or his buyer, for instance a consumer who has bought the thing in a shop) has started to use the goods, perhaps after breaking a sealed package, the product is no longer new, but second hand. Does this prevent the buyer from making valid restitution? The answer, which is no, is found in article 82 (2) letter c). This paragraph makes an exception and states that «if the goods or part of the goods have been sold in the normal course of business or have been consumed or transformed by the buyer in the course of normal use before he discovered or ought to have discovered the lack of conformity».

We have seen from CISG articles 82 (2) and 84 (2) that the buyer is granted a right to declare avoidance/require substitute goods even if he has used the goods. Article 82 (2) letter c) grants the buyer this right also when he has sold the goods «in the normal course of business». The lack of conformity is, for instance, not discovered until the second buyer has started to use the goods he bought from the first buyer. This second buyer may then be entitled to declare avoidance/require substitute goods from the first buyer, who in turn may raise claims according to the CISG against the seller. Of course, the ordinary conditions in the CISG have to be met. The lack of conformity has to exist at the time when the risk passes to the buyer, see article 36. And there must not exist any reason why the first buyer ought to have discovered it during the time he held the goods before he delivered it to the new buyer, see article 39 (1).

There are also a few other exceptions to the prerequisite that the buyer has to make restitution of the goods substantially in the condition he received them, see article 82 letters a) and b). Letter b) makes an exception «if the goods or part of the goods have perished or deteriorated as a result of the examination provided for in article 38». The buyer has for instance opened the sealed package and/or made the goods subject to ordinary testing. Such activities are to be accepted as long as they are required by article 38 in order to discover lack of conformity.

CISG article 82 (2) letter a) makes an exception if the required quality of restitution is made impossible due to other factors than the buyer's act or omission. This article is in fact an exception from the passing of the risk regulated in CISG chapter IV (articles 66 to 70). It is also in accordance with article 70 which states that the articles about passing of the risk (articles 67, 68 and 69) «do not impair the remedies available to the buyer on account of the breach» ... «if the seller has committed a fundamental breach of contract». And a fundamental breach is exactly what is the case when the buyer is entitled to declare avoidance/require substitute goods, see articles 49 (1) and 46 (2).

These regulations are reasonable. When the goods seriously suffer from a lack of conformity, the seller in breach should not be allowed to benefit from the articles about the passing of the risk and thus refer the consequences of accidents damaging the goods over to the buyer – provided that the buyer has not by his acts or omissions made the accidents possible. If such accidents damage the goods the buyer may declare the contract avoided/require substitute goods even if he is now – after the damaging accident – no longer able to make restitution of the goods substantially in the same condition in which he received them, see article 82 (2) letter a) and also article 80. These articles apply if the goods, for example, burn or are stolen in circumstances where the buyer is not to blame. They also apply if fresh goods naturally deteriorate even if they are properly stored, or if the goods are installed into a building and suffer damage when they are taken out.

7.4 Anticipatory breach.

CISG chapter V Section I concerns anticipatory breach. The question here is what remedies are available if there are good reasons to fear – already before the obligation is due – that one party eventually will fail to perform according to the contract. Articles 71 and 72 have a wide sphere of application: These provisions are common to the obligations of both the seller and the buyer, as expressed in the headline above these articles in the convention.

Nevertheless I have chosen two practical situations to comment on; delayed or no delivery of the goods from the seller and delayed or no payment from the buyer.

As far as *delayed or no delivery* of the goods is concerned, it is a practical question whether or not the buyer may declare the contract avoided according to article 49 already *before* the time of delivery has come. There could be several reasons that make it clear that the seller will not be able to deliver in time:

The seller himself may have said that he does not intend to deliver. Impediments could have occurred that make delivery impossible, like fire in the seller's factory or export or import bans from the governmental authorities. Or the seller's financial situation may have deteriorated to a degree that gives reasons to fear delivery difficulties. In such situations it would be a big disadvantage for the buyer to have to wait – not only for the time of delivery – but also until the time of delivery is *fundamentally* exceeded, as required by article 49, before he can declare the contract avoided.

As article 72 makes it possible to declare the contract avoided as soon as a breach is expected, the buyer can start earlier to try to get the goods he needs from a different seller or manage the situation otherwise. The buyer's loss will thus be smaller. The seller will benefit from this because the buyer's damage claims will then be reduced according to the damage provisions in article 45 (1) letter b) and articles 74-77.

The buyer can only declare the contract avoided at such an early point if it is very likely that the seller's delivery will be fundamentally delayed: Article 72 requires that «it is clear that one of the parties will commit a fundamental breach of contract».

A high degree of probability is needed in order to entitle the buyer to avoid the contract due to anticipatory breach. This is important in order to protect the seller from ungrounded claims from the buyer. If time allows, the buyer must according to article 72 (2) «give reasonable notice to the other party in order to permit him to provide adequate assurance of his performance». As indicated in this article it may be necessary to make a quick decision, and here we have to consider the probability. If it is sufficiently clear (see the conditions in article 72) that a fundamental breach will occur, it does not matter if the seller, despite a bad forecast, should still be able to deliver.

Let us now take a look at the case of *delayed payment*. For a seller it is important to act early to prevent losses. If it becomes apparent that the buyer will not pay the price according to the contract, the seller may suspend the delivery, see article 71. Although the seller according to article 58 (1) 2nd sentence may refuse to hand over the goods unless they are paid for, he will in many cases benefit from the opportunity to take action earlier. Here the seller may rely on article 71. When it comes to contracts for the supply of goods to be manufactured or produced, the seller has to stop the production in time to avoid losses that the buyer may not be able to pay for.

To make the seller entitled to suspend delivery, article 71 requires a certain probability that the buyer will fail to pay; it must become «apparent that the other party will not perform a substantial part of his obligations as a result of:

(a) a serious deficiency in his ability to perform or in his creditworthiness; or

(b) his conduct in preparing to perform or in performing the contract».

Article 71 applies to suspending of performance. Here it must become *apparent* that the other party will fail to perform. In article 72 the probability must be even greater; here it has to become *clear* that such a failure will occur. «Clear» is a stronger word than «apparent» in the same way as avoiding the contract is a stronger remedy than suspending it.

7.5 Instalment contracts. Breach of a part

CISG article 73 applies to contracts for delivery of goods by instalments – in general – whether the delivery of goods or the payment or both are to be presented in instalments.

Article 51 applies when instalments are not agreed upon, and only a part of the goods are delivered in conformity with the contract. If part of the goods are delivered too late or not delivered at all, the buyer may keep the goods he has received and make claims according to articles 46 to 50 for the part that is delivered too late/not delivered, see article 51 (1). If the buyer instead chooses to have the contract avoided, according to article 81, he has to make restitution of the goods he has received, and the breach in total has to be fundamental, see article 51 (2). In order to decide on fundamental breach we have to consider how severely the buyer is hit by the seller's breach of contract: Is it important for the buyer to receive the goods, and in time? Does it count for a substantial part of the contract? We have to see the contract as a whole. Does the seller offer to compensate in any way for costs and inconvenience? The question of fundamental breach in the CISG is to be decided according to article 25.

The considerations above are similar if all the goods are delivered, but a part of the delivered goods does not conform with the contract.

If delivery in part is agreed upon we have an instalment contract and article 73 applies. It states: «If the failure of one party to perform any of his obligations in respect of any instalment constitutes a fundamental breach of contract with respect to that instalment, the other party may declare the contract avoided with respect to that instalment». This article refers to breach of contract both by the seller and by the buyer. If the seller, for example, fails to deliver one of the instalments in time, and this breach of contract for that specific instalment is fundamental (see article 25 again), the buyer may cancel that specific instalment. If, however, the same seller's breach of contract for one instalment gives good reasons to fear for the future instalments, article 73 (2) applies:

«If one party's failure to perform any of his obligations in respect of any instalment gives the other party good grounds to conclude that a fundamental breach of contract will occur with respect to future instalments, he may declare the contract avoided for the future, provided that he does so within a reasonable time».

Article 73 (2), like article 73 (1), applies to all types of breach of contract both by the seller and the buyer. For example, the buyer's failure to pay one instalment in due time may often give «good grounds to conclude» that the buyer is in a severe financial condition and is therefore not likely to be able to pay according to the contract for the future instalments either.

If the buyer declares the contract avoided in respect of any delivery, he may, according to article 73 (3), extend the cancellation to «deliveries already made or future deliveries if, by reason of their interdependence, those deliveries could not be used for the purpose contemplated by the parties at the time of the conclusion of the contract». If this is the case the buyer may cancel these other instalments even it they are – or are likely to be - delivered according to the contract. These other instalments only have to be closely interdependent with the instalments suffering from fundamental breach. According to article 73 the buyer may declare avoidance in respect of one or more of these other instalments – if each individual instalment possesses the required degree of interdependence with the instalment(s) in fundamental breach. If all the instalments are closely interdependent, this means that the buyer may declare the whole contract avoided. In this latest case there is likely to be a fundamental breach according to articles 49 and 25, too.

While discussing article 73 we should point out that this article gives the buyer an *option* to cancel the contract – an option he decides by himself if he wants to use or not. According to article 73, a seller who is in breach for a part of the goods cannot force the buyer to use his right to a greater extent than the buyer prefers.

If the contract requires delivery of several items and one or more of the items do not conform with the contract, article 51 applies to the situation. The term «part of the goods» may raise some doubt. It cannot possibly apply to just a single part of a product, for instance a defect component inside a car. The article will apply, however, if one out of the ten delivered cars is defected. Article 51 states that articles 46 to 50 apply to the defected car, deciding what claims the buyer may raise. If these defects amount to fundamental breach, the buyer may declare the contract avoided (as far as the defected car is concerned), see articles 49 and 25. The buyer may not declare the entire contract avoided, if the breach does not amount to a fundamental breach for the contract as a whole, see article 51 (2).

7.6 Preservation of the goods

Most people tend to look after their possessions carefully and see to it that they do not suffer any harm. They do not need a law to motivate them. It is a different situation to be in charge of goods, which one does not own. Therefore the CISG provides articles concerning preservation of the goods. See CISG section VI. During the process of delivering the goods, it may occur that one of the parties *is in possession of the goods, but does not bear the risk of it*. In such cases this party may not trouble himself that much, since it is the other party who has to bear the costs if something was to happen to the goods.

In the CISG we find regulations on preservation of the goods in two such situations:

1) According to article 85 *the seller* must «take such steps as are reasonable in the circumstances to preserve them» if «the buyer is in delay in taking delivery of the goods or, where payment of the price and delivery of the goods are to be made concurrently, if he fails to pay the price». Usually *the buyer* is the party who bears the risk in such cases, according to CISG chapter IV, but nevertheless the seller has to take care of the goods, if he is either «in possession of the goods or otherwise able to control their disposition».

2) According to article 86, *the buyer* must «take such steps to preserve [the goods] as are reasonable in the circumstances» if «the buyer has received the goods and intends to exercise any right under the contract or this Convention to reject them». The *seller* is usually the party who bears the risk in such cases, according to CISG article 70, but nevertheless the buyer still has to take care of the goods.

The implications of the preservation duty are the same for both of the cases above. The party who is in possession of the goods and therefore has to «take such steps as are reasonable in the circumstances to preserve» the goods, has the right to be «reimbursed his reasonable expenses» by the other party, see articles 85 and 86 (1). It is not easy to say much in general about what to consider reasonable steps. This will obviously depend on the goods and the situation as a whole.

If the other party – the party who owns the goods but is not in charge of them at the moment – eventually wants to receive them, he will first have to pay for the preservation expenses, see both article 85 and article 86 (1).

Even if this other party may have lost interest in the goods by now, he still has to pay for their preservation, even to a third party with whom the goods are now *deposited*, see article 87.

Eventually the party who happens to possess the goods may sell them and retain «an amount equal to the reasonable expenses of preserving the goods and of selling them», see article 88 (3), which also requires «account to the other party for the balance». However, in this sale article 88 (1) and (2) have to be observed. The party selling the goods must give notice to the other party (the contract party bearing the risk for the goods). This notice must be reasonable, see article 88 (1), and to the extent possible «give notice to the other party of his intention to sell», see article 88 (2). The sale of the goods must be undertaken «by any appropriate means» and after «there has been an unreasonable delay by the other party in taking possession of the goods or in taking them back or in paying the price or the cost of preservation».

According to article 88 (2), if «the goods are subject to rapid deterioration or their preservation would involve unreasonable expense», the party in accidental possession of the goods is not only *allowed* to sell them. Now he *must* «take reasonable measures to sell them», in order to prevent unnecessary waste of values.

CISG Index

Article:	Pages:
1	13
2	13-14
3	13-17
6	18
7	31, 103-106
8	21-22, 31, 37, 57, 66, 68-69
9	18-19, 27, 66
11	27
14	19
15	20
16	20-21
18	19-21
19	19
22	20
23	19
24	20
25	41-42, 76-77, 79, 83-84, 95, 115-117
27	79
28	73

Article:	Pages:
29	73
30	25, 37
31	23, 26, 36
32	27
33	31-32, 38
34	31-32
35	25-26, 56, 58-60, 66-68, 107
36	23, 62-64, 108, 111
37	108
38	67-70, 107-108, 111
39	62, 65, 67-68, 74-75, 84-85, 103-104, 106, 108-109, 111
40	59, 67-68, 109
41	90-91
42	90-91
43	91, 104, 106
44	91
45	25, 38, 39-40, 56, 71, 76, 78, 86, 99, 113
46	39-40, 71-75, 80, 83, 105-106, 111, 115
47	43-44, 75, 79, 85, 96
48	43-44, 72-73, 76-80, 83-85, 106

Article:	Pages:
49	40-51, 74-86, 95, 105-106, 111-113, 116-117
50	72, 74, 78-81
51	114-116, 117
52	38
53	28, 97
54	28, 97
55	33
57	33-34
58	34-35, 94, 114
60	28, 72
61	34, 93, 99
62	94
63	96
64	34, 95-97, 105-106
65	97
66	24-26, 30
67	23, 26-29, 108, 111
68	30-31, 111
69	28, 111
70	29, 111, 118

Article:	Pages:
71	28, 35, 37, 112, 114
72	37, 112-114
73	114-116
74	86, 96-97, 99-100, 109
75	41, 86, 96, 100-102
76	100-102
77	55, 79, 102-103
78	34, 94, 105
79	34, 45-55, 86-89, 92, 97, 109
80	71, 93
81	41, 81, 90, 120-121, 123
82	29-30, 74, 110-112
84	110-111
85	98, 117-118
86	117-118
87	118
88	118-119
92	21

Literature

Viggo Hagstrøm and Magnus Aarbakke: Obligasjonsrett, 2003

Kai Krüger, Norsk kjøpsrett, 1999

J. Lookofsky, Understanding the CISG in Scandinavia, 1996

J. Lookofsky, Understanding the CISG in the USA, 1995

Roald Martinussen, Kjøpsrett, 2004

Larry A DiMatteo et al., International Sales Law : A Critical Analysis of CISG Jurisprudence, 2005

Jan Ramberg and Johnny Herre, Internationella köplagen (CISG) En kommentar, 2001.

P. Schlechtriem (ed.), Commentary on the UN Convention on the International Sale of Goods, 1998

Appendix

United Nations Convention on Contracts for the International Sale of Goods (1980)

Preamble. The States Parties to this Convention, *Bearing in Mind* the broad objectives in the resolutions adopted by the sixth special session of the General Assembly of the United Nations on the establishment of a New International Economic Order, *Considering* that the development of international trade on the basis of equality and mutual benefit is an important element in promoting friendly relations among States, *Being of the Opinion* that the adoption of uniform rules which govern contracts for the international sale of goods and

take into account the different social, economic and legal systems would contribute to the removal of legal barriers in international trade and promote the development of international trade, have decreed as follows:

PART I
Sphere of Application and General Provisions

Chapter I
Sphere of Application

Article 1
(1) This Convention applies to contracts of sale of goods between parties whose places of business are in different States:
(a) when the States are Contracting States; or
(b) when the rules of private international law lead to the application of the law of a Contracting State.
(2) The fact that the parties have their places of business in different States is to be disregarded whenever this fact does not
appear either from the contract or from any dealings between, or from information disclosed by, the parties at any time before
or at the conclusion of the contract.
(3) Neither the nationality of the parties nor the civil or commercial character of the parties or of the contract is to be taken into
consideration in determining the application of this Convention.

Article 2
This Convention does not apply to sales:
(a) of goods bought for personal, family or household use, unless the seller, at any time before or at the conclusion of the
contract, neither knew nor ought to have known that the goods were bought for any such use;
(b) by auction;
(c) on execution or otherwise by authority of law;
(d) of stocks, shares, investment securities, negotiable instruments or money;

(e) of ships, vessels, hovercraft or aircraft;
(f) of electricity.

Article 3
(1) Contracts for the supply of goods to be manufactured or produced are to be considered sales unless the party who orders the goods undertakes to supply a substantial part of the materials necessary for such manufacture or production.
(2) This Convention does not apply to contracts in which the preponderant part of the obligations of the party who furnishes the goods consists in the supply of labour or other services.

Article 4
This Convention governs only the formation of the contract of sale and the rights and obligations of the seller and the buyer arising from such a contract. In particular, except as otherwise expressly provided in this Convention, it is not concerned with:
(a) the validity of the contract or of any of its provisions or of any usage;
(b) the effect which the contract may have on the property in the goods sold.

Article 5
This Convention does not apply to the liability of the seller for death or personal injury caused by the goods to any person.

Article 6
The parties may exclude the application of this Convention or, subject to article 12, derogate from or vary the effect of any of its provisions.

Chapter II
General Provisions

Article 7
(1) In the interpretation of this Convention, regard is to be had to its international character and to the need to promote uniformity in its application and the observance of good faith in international trade.
(2) Questions concerning matters governed by this Convention which are not expressly settled in it are to be settled in conformity with the general principles on which it is based or, in the absence of such principles, in conformity with the law applicable by virtue of the rules of private international law.

Article 8
(1) For the purposes of this Convention statements made by and other conduct of a party are to be interpreted according to his intent where the other party knew or could not have been unaware what that intent was.
(2) If the preceding paragraph is not applicable, statements made by and other conduct of a party are to be interpreted according to the understanding that a reasonable person of the same kind as the other party would have had in the same circumstances.
(3) In determining the intent of a party or the understanding a reasonable person would have had, due consideration is to be given to all relevant circumstances of the case

including the negotiations, any practices which the parties have established between themselves, usages and any subsequent conduct of the parties.

Article 9
(1) The parties are bound by any usage to which they have agreed and by any practices which they have established between themselves.
(2) The parties are considered, unless otherwise agreed, to have impliedly made applicable to their contract or its formation a usage of which the parties knew or ought to have known and which in international trade is widely known to, and regularly observed by, parties to contracts of the type involved in the particular trade concerned.

Article 10
For the purposes of this Convention:
(a) if a party has more than one place of business, the place of business is that which has the closest relationship to the contract and its performance, having regard to the circumstances known to or contemplated by the parties at any time before or at the conclusion of the contract;
(b) if a party does not have a place of business, reference is to be made to his habitual residence.

Article 11
A contract of sale need not be concluded in or evidenced by writing and is not subject to any other requirement as to form. It may be proved by any means, including witnesses.

Article 12
Any provision of article 11, article 29 or Part II of this Convention that allows a contract of sale or its modification or termination by agreement or any offer, acceptance or other indication of intention to be made in any form other than in writing does not apply where any party has his place of business in a Contracting State which has made a declaration under article 96 of this Convention. The parties may not derogate from or vary the effect or this article.

Article 13
For the purposes of this Convention "writing" includes telegram and telex.

PART II
Formation of the Contract

Article 14
(1) A proposal for concluding a contract addressed to one or more specific persons constitutes an offer if it is sufficiently definite and indicates the intention of the offeror to be bound in case of acceptance. A proposal is sufficiently definite if it indicates the goods and expressly or implicitly fixes or makes provision for determining the quantity and the price.
(2) A proposal other than one addressed to one or more specific persons is to be considered merely as an invitation to make offers, unless the contrary is clearly indicated by the person making the proposal.

Article 15

(1) An offer becomes effective when it reaches the offeree.
(2) An offer, even if it is irrevocable, may be withdrawn if the withdrawal reaches the offeree before or at the same time as the
offer.

Article 16

(1) Until a contract is concluded an offer may be revoked if the revocation reaches the offeree before he has dispatched an acceptance.
(2) However, an offer cannot be revoked:
(a) if it indicates, whether by stating a fixed time for acceptance or otherwise, that it is irrevocable; or
(b) if it was reasonable for the offeree to rely on the offer as being irrevocable and the offeree has acted in reliance on the offer.

Article 17

An offer, even if it is irrevocable, is terminated when a rejection reaches the offeror.

Article 18

(1) A statement made by or other conduct of the offeree indicating assent to an offer is an acceptance. Silence or inactivity does not in itself amount to acceptance.
(2) An acceptance of an offer becomes effective at the moment the indication of assent reaches the offeror. An acceptance is not effective if the indication of assent does not reach the offeror within the time he has fixed or, if no time is fixed, within a reasonable time, due account being taken of the circumstances of the transaction, including the rapidity of the means of communication employed by the offeror. An oral offer must be accepted immediately unless the circumstances indicate otherwise.
(3) However, if, by virtue of the offer or as a result of practices which the parties have established between themselves or of usage, the offeree may indicate assent by performing an act, such as one relating to the dispatch of the goods or payment of the price, without notice to the offeror, the acceptance is effective at the moment the act is performed, provided that the act is performed within the period of time laid down in the preceding paragraph.

Article 19

(1) A reply to an offer which purports to be an acceptance but contains additions, limitations or other modifications is a rejection of the offer and constitutes a counter-offer.
(2) However, a reply to an offer which purports to be an acceptance but contains additional or different terms which do not materially alter the terms of the offer constitutes an acceptance, unless the offeror, without undue delay, objects orally to the discrepancy or dispatches a notice to that effect. If he does not so object, the terms of the contract are the terms of the offer with the modifications contained in the acceptance.
(3) Additional or different terms relating, among other things, to the price, payment, quality and quantity of the goods, place and time of delivery, extent of one party's liability to the other or the settlement of disputes are considered to alter the terms of the offer materially.

Article 20

(1) A period of time for acceptance fixed by the offeror in a telegram or a letter begins to run from the moment the telegram is handed in for dispatch or from the date shown on the letter or, if no such date is shown, from the date shown on the envelope. A period of time for acceptance fixed by the offeror by telephone, telex or other means of instantaneous communication, begins to run from the moment that the offer reaches the offeree.

(2) Official holidays or non-business days occurring during the period for acceptance are included in calculating the period. However, if a notice of acceptance cannot be delivered at the address of the offeror on the last day of the period because that day falls on an official holiday or a non-business day at the place of business of the offeror, the period is extended until the first business day which follows.

Article 21

(1) A late acceptance is nevertheless effective as an acceptance if without delay the offeror orally so informs the offeree or dispatches a notice to that effect.

(2) If a letter or other writing containing a late acceptance shows that it has been sent in such circumstances that if its transmission had been normal it would have reached the offeror in due time, the late acceptance is effective as an acceptance unless, without delay, the offeror orally informs the offeree that he considers his offer as having lapsed or dispatches a notice to that effect.

Article 22

An acceptance may be withdrawn if the withdrawal reaches the offeror before or at the same time as the acceptance would have become effective.

Article 23

A contract is concluded at the moment when an acceptance of an offer becomes effective in accordance with the provisions of this Convention.

Article 24

For the purposes of this Part of the Convention, an offer, declaration of acceptance or any other indication of intention "reaches" the addressee when it is made orally to him or delivered by any other means to him personally, to his place of business or mailing address or, if he does not have a place of business or mailing address, to his habitual residence.

PART III
Sale of Goods

Chapter I
General Provisions

Article 25

A breach of contract committed by one of the parties is fundamental if it results in such detriment to the other party as substantially to deprive him of what he is entitled to expect under the contract, unless the party in breach did not foresee and a reasonable person of the same kind in the same circumstances would not have foreseen such a result.

Article 26
A declaration of avoidance of the contract is effective only if made by notice to the other party.

Article 27
Unless otherwise expressly provided in this Part of the Convention, if any notice, request or other communication is given or made by a party in accordance with this Part and by means appropriate in the circumstances, a delay or error in the transmission of the communication or its failure to arrive does not deprive that party of the right to rely on the communication.

Article 28
If, in accordance with the provisions of this Convention, one party is entitled to require performance of any obligation by the other party, a court is not bound to enter a judgement for specific performance unless the court would do so under its own law in respect of similar contracts of sale not governed by this Convention.

Article 29
(1) A contract may be modified or terminated by the mere agreement of the parties.
(2) A contract in writing which contains a provision requiring any modification or termination by agreement to be in writing may not be otherwise modified or terminated by agreement. However, a party may be precluded by his conduct from asserting such a provision to the extent that the other party has relied on that conduct.

Chapter II
Obligations of the Seller

Article 30
The seller must deliver the goods, hand over any documents relating to them and transfer the property in the goods, as required by the contract and this Convention.

Section I. Delivery of the goods and handing over of documents

Article 31
If the seller is not bound to deliver the goods at any other particular place, his obligation to deliver consists:
(a) if the contract of sale involves carriage of the goods - in handing the goods over to the first carrier for transmission to the buyer;
(b) if, in cases not within the preceding subparagraph, the contract related to specific goods, or unidentified goods to be drawn from a specific stock or to be manufactured or produced, and at the time of the conclusion of the contract the parties knew that the goods were at, or were to be manufactured or produced at, a particular place - in placing the goods at the buyer's disposal at that place;

(c) in other cases - in placing the goods at the buyer's disposal at the place where the seller had his place of business at the time of the conclusion of the contract.

Article 32
(1) If the seller, in accordance with the contract or this Convention, hands the goods over to a carrier and if the goods are not clearly identified to the contract by markings on the goods, by shipping documents or otherwise, the seller must give the buyer notice of the consignment specifying the goods.
(2) If the seller is bound to arrange for carriage of the goods, he must make such contracts as are necessary for carriage to the place fixed by means of transportation appropriate in the circumstances and according to the usual terms for such transportation.

(3) If the seller is not bound to effect insurance in respect of the carriage of the goods, he must, at the buyer's request, provide him with all available information necessary to enable him to effect such insurance.

Article 33
The seller must deliver the goods:
(a) if a date is fixed by or determinable from the contract, on that date;
(b) if a period of time is fixed by or determinable from the contract, at any time within that period unless circumstances indicate that the buyer is to choose a date; or
(c) in any other case, within a reasonable time after the conclusion of the contract.

Article 34
If the seller is bound to hand over documents relating to the goods, he must hand them over at the time and place and in the form required by the contract. If the seller has handed over documents before that time, he may, up to that time, cure any lack of conformity in the documents, if the exercise of this right does not cause the buyer unreasonable inconvenience or unreasonable expense. However, the buyer retains any right to claim damages as provided for in this Convention.

Section II. Conformity of the goods and third party claims

Article 35
(1) The seller must deliver goods which are of the quantity, quality and description required by the contract and which are contained or packaged in the manner required by the contract.
(2) Except where the parties have agreed otherwise, the goods do not conform with the contract unless they:
(a) are fit for the purposes for which goods of the same description would ordinarily be used;
(b) are fit for any particular purpose expressly or impliedly made known to the seller at the time of the conclusion of the contract, except where the circumstances show that the buyer did not rely, or that it was unreasonable for him to rely, on the seller's skill and judgement;
(c) possess the qualities of goods which the seller has held out to the buyer as a sample or model;
(d) are contained or packaged in the manner usual for such goods or, where there is no such manner, in a manner adequate to preserve and protect the goods.

(3) The seller is not liable under subparagraphs (a) to (d) of the preceding paragraph for any lack of conformity of the goods if at the time of the conclusion of the contract the buyer knew or could not have been unaware of such lack of conformity.

Article 36

(1) The seller is liable in accordance with the contract and this Convention for any lack of conformity which exists at the time when the risk passes to the buyer, even though the lack of conformity becomes apparent only after that time.
(2) The seller is also liable for any lack of conformity which occurs after the time indicated in the preceding paragraph and which is due to a breach of any of his obligations, including a breach of any guarantee that for a period of time the goods will remain fit for their ordinary purpose or for some particular purpose or will retain specified qualities or characteristics.

Article 37

If the seller has delivered goods before the date for delivery, he may, up to that date, deliver any missing part or make up any deficiency in the quantity of the goods delivered, or deliver goods in replacement of any non-conforming goods delivered or remedy any lack of conformity in the goods delivered, provided that the exercise of this right does not cause the buyer unreasonable inconvenience or unreasonable expense. However, the buyer retains any right to claim damages as provided for in this Convention.

Article 38

(1) The buyer must examine the goods, or cause them to be examined, within as short a period as is practicable in the circumstances.
(2) If the contract involves carriage of the goods, examination may be deferred until after the goods have arrived at their destination.
(3) If the goods are redirected in transit or redispatched by the buyer without a reasonable opportunity for examination by him and at the time of the conclusion of the contract the seller knew or ought to have known of the possibility of such redirection or redispatch, examination may be deferred until after the goods have arrived at the new destination.

Article 39

(1) The buyer loses the right to rely on a lack of conformity of the goods if he does not give notice to the seller specifying the nature of the lack of conformity within a reasonable time after he has discovered it or ought to have discovered it.
(2) In any event, the buyer loses the right to rely on a lack of conformity of the goods if he does not give the seller notice thereof at the latest within a period of two years from the date on which the goods were actually handed over to the buyer, unless this time-limit is inconsistent with a contractual period of guarantee.

Article 40

The seller is not entitled to rely on the provisions of articles 38 and 39 if the lack of conformity relates to facts of which he knew or could not have been unaware and which he did not disclose to the buyer.

Article 41

The seller must deliver goods which are free from any right or claim of a third party, unless the buyer agreed to take the goods subject to that right or claim. However, if such right or claim is based on industrial property or other intellectual property, the seller's obligation is governed by article 42.

Article 42

(1) The seller must deliver goods which are free from any right or claim of a third party based on industrial property or other intellectual property, of which at the time of the conclusion of the contract the seller knew or could not have been unaware,
provided that the right or claim is based on industrial property or other intellectual property:
(a) under the law of the State where the goods will be resold or otherwise used, if it was contemplated by the parties at the time of the conclusion of the contract that the goods would be resold or otherwise used in that State; or
(b) in any other case, under the law of the State where the buyer has his place of business.
(2) The obligation of the seller under the preceding paragraph does not extend to cases where:
(a) at the time of the conclusion of the contract the buyer knew or could not have been unaware of the right or claim; or
(b) the right or claim results from the seller's compliance with technical drawings, designs, formulae or other such specifications furnished by the buyer.

Article 43

(1) The buyer loses the right to rely on the provisions of article 41 or Article 42 if he does not give notice to the seller specifying the nature of the right or claim of the third party within a reasonable time after he has become aware or ought to have become aware of the right or claim.
(2) The seller is not entitled to rely on the provisions of the preceding paragraph if he knew of the right or claim of the third party and the nature of it.

Article 44

Notwithstanding the provisions of paragraph (1) of article 39 and paragraph (1) of article 43, the buyer may reduce the price in accordance with Article 50 or claim damages, except for loss of profit, if he has a reasonable excuse for his failure to give the required notice.

Section III. Remedies for breach of contract by the seller

Article 45

(1) If the seller fails to perform any of his obligations under the contract or this Convention, the buyer may:
(a) exercise the rights provided in articles 46 to 52;
(b) claim damages as provided in articles 74 to 77.
(2) The buyer is not deprived of any right he may have to claim damages by exercising his right to other remedies.
(3) No period of grace may be granted to the seller by a court or arbitral tribunal when the buyer resorts to a remedy for breach of contract.

Article 46

(1) The buyer may require performance by the seller of his obligations unless the buyer

has resorted to a remedy which is inconsistent with this requirement.

(2) If the goods do not conform with the contract, the buyer may require delivery of substitute goods only if the lack of conformity constitutes a fundamental breach of contract and a request for substitute goods is made either in conjunction with notice given under article 39 or within a reasonable time thereafter.

(3) If the goods do not conform with the contract, the buyer may require the seller to remedy the lack of conformity by repair, unless this is unreasonable having regard to all the circumstances. A request for repair must be made either in conjunction with notice given under article 39 or within a reasonable time thereafter.

Article 47

(1) The buyer may fix an additional period of time of reasonable length for performance by the seller of his obligations.

(2) Unless the buyer has received notice from the seller that he will not perform within the period so fixed, the buyer may not, during that period, resort to any remedy for breach of contract. However, the buyer is not deprived thereby of any right he may have to claim damages for delay in performance.

Article 48

(1) Subject to article 49, the seller may, even after the date for delivery, remedy at his own expense any failure to perform his obligations, if he can do so without unreasonable delay and without causing the buyer unreasonable inconvenience or uncertainty of reimbursement by the seller of expenses advanced by the buyer. However, the buyer retains any right to claim damages as provided for in this Convention.

(2) If the seller requests the buyer to make known whether he will accept performance and the buyer does not comply with the request within a reasonable time, the seller may perform within the time indicated in his request. The buyer may not, during that period of time, resort to any remedy which is inconsistent with performance by the seller.

(3) A notice by the seller that he will perform within a specified period of time is assumed to include a request, under the preceding paragraph, that the buyer make known his decision.

(4) A request or notice by the seller under paragraph (2) or (3) of this Article is not effective unless received by the buyer.

Article 49

(1) The buyer may declare the contract avoided:

(a) if the failure by the seller to perform any of his obligations under the contract or this Convention amounts to a fundamental breach of contract; or

(b) in case of non-delivery, if the seller does not deliver the goods within the additional period of time fixed by the buyer in accordance with paragraph (1) of article 47 or declares that he will not deliver within the period so fixed.

(2) However, in cases where the seller has delivered the goods, the buyer loses the right to declare the contract avoided unless he does so:

(a) in respect of late delivery, within a reasonable time after he has become aware that delivery has been made;

(b) in respect of any breach other than late delivery, within a reasonable time:

(i) after he knew or ought to have known of the breach;

(ii) after the expiration of any additional period of time fixed by the buyer in accordance with paragraph (1) of article 47, or after the seller has declared that he will not perform his obligations within such an additional period; or

(iii) after the expiration of any additional period of time indicated by the seller in accordance with paragraph (2) of article 48, or after the buyer has declared that he will not accept performance.

Article 50
If the goods do not conform with the contract and whether or not the price has already been paid, the buyer may reduce the price in the same proportion as the value that the goods actually delivered had at the time of the delivery bears to the value that conforming goods would have had at that time. However, if the seller remedies any failure to perform his obligations in accordance with article 37 or article 48 or if the buyer refuses to accept performance by the seller in accordance with those Articles, the buyer may not reduce the price.

Article 51
(1) If the seller delivers only a part of the goods or if only a part of the goods delivered is in conformity with the contract, articles 46 to 50 apply in respect of the part which is missing or which does not conform.
(2) The buyer may declare the contract avoided in its entirety only if the failure to make delivery completely or in conformity with the contract amounts to a fundamental breach of the contract.

Article 52
(1) If the seller delivers the goods before the date fixed, the buyer may take delivery or refuse to take delivery.
(2) If the seller delivers a quantity of goods greater than that provided for in the contract, the buyer may take delivery or refuse to take delivery of the excess quantity. If the buyer takes delivery of all or part of the excess quantity, he must pay for it at the contract rate.

Chapter III
Obligations of the Buyer

Article 53
The buyer must pay the price for the goods and take delivery of them as required by the contract and this Convention.

Section I. Payment of the price

Article 54
The buyer's obligation to pay the price includes taking such steps and complying with such formalities as may be required under the contract or any laws and regulations to enable payment to be made.

Article 55
Where a contract has been validly concluded but does not expressly or implicitly fix or make provision for determining the price, the parties are considered, in the absence of any indication to the contrary, to have impliedly made reference to the price generally

charged at the time of the conclusion of the contract for such goods sold under comparable circumstances in the trade concerned.

Article 56
If the price is fixed according to the weight of the goods, in case of doubt it is to be determined by the net weight.

Article 57
(1) If the buyer is not bound to pay the price at any other particular place, he must pay it to the seller:
(a) at the seller's place of business; or
(b) if the payment is to be made against the handing over of the goods or of documents, at the place where the handing over takes place.
(2) The seller must bear any increases in the expenses incidental to payment which is caused by a change in his place of business subsequent to the conclusion of the contract.

Article 58
(1) If the buyer is not bound to pay the price at any other specific time, he must pay it when the seller places either the goods or documents controlling their disposition at the buyer's disposal in accordance with the contract and this Convention. The seller may make such payment a condition for handing over the goods or documents.
(2) If the contract involves carriage of the goods, the seller may dispatch the goods on terms whereby the goods, or documents controlling their disposition, will not be handed over to the buyer except against payment of the price.
(3) The buyer is not bound to pay the price until he has had an opportunity to examine the goods, unless the procedures for delivery or payment agreed upon by the parties are inconsistent with his having such an opportunity.

Article 59
The buyer must pay the price on the date fixed by or determinable from the contract and this Convention without the need for any request or compliance with any formality on the part of the seller.

Section II. Taking delivery

Article 60
The buyer's obligation to take delivery consists:
(a) in doing all the acts which could reasonably be expected of him in order to enable the seller to make delivery; and
(b) in taking over the goods.

Section III. Remedies for breach of contract by the buyer

Article 61
(1) If the buyer fails to perform any of his obligations under the contract or this Convention, the seller may:
(a) exercise the rights provided in articles 62 to 65;
(b) claim damages as provided in articles 74 to 77.
(2) The seller is not deprived of any right he may have to claim damages by exercising

his right to other remedies.

(3) No period of grace may be granted to the buyer by a court or arbitral tribunal when the seller resorts to a remedy for breach of contract.

Article 62

The seller may require the buyer to pay the price, take delivery or perform his other obligations, unless the seller has resorted to a remedy which is inconsistent with this requirement.

Article 63

(1) The seller may fix an additional period of time of reasonable length for performance by the buyer of his obligations.

(2) Unless the seller has received notice from the buyer that he will not perform within the period so fixed, the seller may not, during that period, resort to any remedy for breach of contract. However, the seller is not deprived thereby of any right he may have to claim damages for delay in performance.

Article 64

(1) The seller may declare the contract avoided:

(a) if the failure by the buyer to perform any of his obligations under the contract or this Convention amounts to a fundamental breach of contract; or

(b) if the buyer does not, within the additional period of time fixed by the seller in accordance with paragraph (1) of article 63, perform his obligation to pay the price or take delivery of the goods, or if he declares that he will not do so within the period so fixed.

(2) However, in cases where the buyer has paid the price, the seller loses the right to declare the contract avoided unless he does so:

(a) in respect of late performance by the buyer, before the seller has become aware that performance has been rendered; or

(b) in respect of any breach other than late performance by the buyer, within a reasonable time:

(i) after the seller knew or ought to have known of the breach; or

(ii) after the expiration of any additional period of time fixed by the seller in accordance with paragraph (1) or article 63, or after the buyer has declared that he will not perform his obligations within such an additional period.

Article 65

(1) If under the contract the buyer is to specify the form, measurement or other features of the goods and he fails to make such specification either on the date agreed upon or within a reasonable time after receipt of a request from the seller, the seller may, without prejudice to any other rights he may have, make the specification himself in accordance with the requirements of the buyer that may be known to him.

(2) If the seller makes the specification himself, he must inform the buyer of the details thereof and must fix a reasonable time within which the buyer may make a different specification. If, after receipt of such a communication, the buyer fails to do so within the time so fixed, the specification made by the seller is binding.

Chapter IV
Passing of Risk

Article 66
Loss of or damage to the goods after the risk has passed to the buyer does not discharge him from his obligation to pay the price, unless the loss or damage is due to an act or omission of the seller.

Article 67
(1) If the contract of sale involves carriage of the goods and the seller is not bound to hand them over at a particular place, the risk passes to the buyer when the goods are handed over to the first carrier for transmission to the buyer in accordance with the contract of sale. If the seller is bound to hand the goods over to a carrier at a particular place, the risk does not pass to the buyer until the goods are handed over to the carrier at that place. The fact that the seller is authorized to retain documents controlling the disposition of the goods does not affect the passage of the risk.
(2) Nevertheless, the risk does not pass to the buyer until the goods are clearly identified to the contract, whether by markings on the goods, by shipping documents, by notice given to the buyer or otherwise.

Article 68
The risk in respect of goods sold in transit passes to the buyer from the time of the conclusion of the contract. However, if the circumstances so indicate, the risk is assumed by the buyer from the time the goods were handed over to the carrier who issued the documents embodying the contract of carriage. Nevertheless, if at the time of the conclusion of the contract of sale the seller knew or ought to have known that the goods had been lost or damaged and did not disclose this to the buyer, the loss or damage is at the risk of the seller.

Article 69
(1) In cases not within articles 67 and 68, the risk passes to the buyer when he takes over the goods or, if he does not do so in due time, from the time when the goods are placed at his disposal and he commits a breach of contract by failing to take delivery.
(2) However, if the buyer is bound to take over the goods at a place other than a place of business of the seller, the risk passes when delivery is due and the buyer is aware of the fact that the goods are placed at his disposal at that place.
(3) If the contract relates to goods not then identified, the goods are considered not to be placed at the disposal of the buyer until they are clearly identified to the contract.

Article 70
If the seller has committed a fundamental breach of contract, articles 67, 68 and 69 do not impair the remedies available to the buyer on account of the breach.

Chapter V
Provisions Common to the Obligations of the Seller and of the Buyer

Section I. Anticipatory breach and instalment contracts

Article 71

(1) A party may suspend the performance of his obligations if, after the conclusion of the contract, it becomes apparent that the other party will not perform a substantial part of his obligations as a result of:

(a) a serious deficiency in his ability to perform or in his creditworthiness; or

(b) his conduct in preparing to perform or in performing the contract.

(2) If the seller has already dispatched the goods before the grounds described in the preceding paragraph become evident, he may prevent the handing over of the goods to the buyer even though the buyer holds a document which entitles him to obtain them. The present paragraph relates only to the rights in the goods as between the buyer and the seller.

(3) A party suspending performance, whether before or after dispatch of the goods, must immediately give notice of the suspension to the other party and must continue with performance if the other party provides adequate assurance of his performance.

Article 72

(1) If prior to the date for performance of the contract it is clear that one of the parties will commit a fundamental breach of contract, the other party may declare the contract avoided.

(2) If time allows, the party intending to declare the contract avoided must give reasonable notice to the other party in order to permit him to provide adequate assurance of his performance.

(3) The requirements of the preceding paragraph do not apply if the other party has declared that he will not perform his obligations.

Article 73

(1) In the case of a contract for delivery of goods by instalments, if the failure of one party to perform any of his obligations in respect of any instalment constitutes a fundamental breach of contract with respect to that instalment, the other party may declare the contract avoided with respect to that instalment.

(2) If one party's failure to perform any of his obligations in respect of any instalment gives the other party good grounds to conclude that a fundamental breach of contract will occur with respect to future instalments, he may declare the contract avoided for the future, provided that he does so within a reasonable time.

(3) A buyer who declares the contract avoided in respect of any delivery may, at the same time, declare it avoided in respect of deliveries already made or of future deliveries if, by reason of their interdependence, those deliveries could not be used for the purpose contemplated by the parties at the time of the conclusion of the contract.

Section II. Damages

Article 74

Damages for breach of contract by one party consist of a sum equal to the loss, including loss of profit, suffered by the other party as a consequence of the breach. Such damages may not exceed the loss which the party in breach foresaw or ought to have foreseen at the time of the conclusion of the contract, in the light of the facts and matters of which he then knew or ought to have known, as a possible consequence of the breach of contract.

Article 75

If the contract is avoided and if, in a reasonable manner and within a reasonable time after avoidance, the buyer has bought goods in replacement or the seller has resold the goods, the party claiming damages may recover the difference between the contract price and the price in the substitute transaction as well as any further damages recoverable under article 74.

Article 76

(1) If the contract is avoided and there is a current price for the goods, the party claiming damages may, if he has not made a purchase or resale under article 75, recover the difference between the price fixed by the contract and the current price at the time of avoidance as well as any further damages recoverable under article 74. If, however, the party claiming damages has avoided the contract after taking over the goods, the current price at the time of such taking over shall be applied instead of the current price at the time of avoidance.

(2) For the purposes of the preceding paragraph, the current price is the price prevailing at the place where delivery of the goods should have been made or, if there is no current price at that place, the price at such other place as serves as a reasonable substitute, making due allowance for differences in the cost of transporting the goods.

Article 77

A party who relies on a breach of contract must take such measures as are reasonable in the circumstances to mitigate the loss, including loss of profit, resulting from the breach. If he fails to take such measures, the party in breach may claim a reduction in the damages in the amount by which the loss should have been mitigated.

Section III. Interest

Article 78

If a party fails to pay the price or any other sum that is in arrears, the other party is entitled to interest on it, without prejudice to any claim for damages recoverable under article 74.

Section IV. Exemptions

Article 79

(1) A party is not liable for a failure to perform any of his obligations if he proves that the failure was due to an impediment beyond his control and that he could not reasonably be expected to have taken the impediment into account at the time of the conclusion of the contract or to have avoided or overcome it or its consequences.

(2) If the party's failure is due to the failure by a third person whom he has engaged to perform the whole or a part of the contract, that party is exempt from liability only if:

(a) he is exempt under the preceding paragraph; and

(b) the person whom he has so engaged would be so exempt if the provisions of that paragraph were applied to him.

(3) The exemption provided by this article has effect for the period during which the impediment exists.

(4) The party who fails to perform must give notice to the other party of the impediment and its effect on his ability to perform. If the notice is not received by the other party within a reasonable time after the party who fails to perform knew or ought to have

known of the impediment, he is liable for damages resulting from such non-receipt.
(5) Nothing in this article prevents either party from exercising any right other than to claim damages under this Convention

Article 80
A party may not rely on a failure of the other party to perform, to the extent that such failure was caused by the first party's act or omission.

Section V. Effects of avoidance

Article 81
(1) Avoidance of the contract releases both parties from their obligations under it, subject to any damages which may be due. Avoidance does not affect any provision of the contract for the settlement of disputes or any other provision of the contract governing the rights and obligations of the parties consequent upon the avoidance of the contract.
(2) A party who has performed the contract either wholly or in part may claim restitution from the other party of whatever the first party has supplied or paid under the contract. If both parties are bound to make restitution, they must do so concurrently.

Article 82
(1) The buyer loses the right to declare the contract avoided or to require the seller to deliver substitute goods if it is impossible for him to make restitution of the goods substantially in the condition in which he received them.
(2) The preceding paragraph does not apply:
(a) if the impossibility of making restitution of the goods or of making restitution of the goods substantially in the condition in which the buyer received them is not due to his act or omission;
(b) if the goods or part of the goods have perished or deteriorated as a result of the examination provided for in article 38; or
(c) if the goods or part of the goods have been sold in the normal course of business or have been consumed or transformed by the buyer in the course of normal use before he discovered or ought to have discovered the lack of conformity.

Article 83
A buyer who has lost the right to declare the contract avoided or to require the seller to deliver substitute goods in accordance with article 82 retains all other remedies under the contract and this Convention.

Article 84
(1) If the seller is bound to refund the price, he must also pay interest on it, from the date on which the price was paid.
(2) The buyer must account to the seller for all benefits which he has derived from the goods or part of them:
(a) if he must make restitution of the goods or part of them; or
(b) if it is impossible for him to make restitution of all or part of the goods or to make restitution of all or part of the goods substantially in the condition in which he received them, but he has nevertheless declared the contract avoided or required the seller to deliver substitute goods.

Section VI. Preservation of the goods

Article 85
If the buyer is in delay in taking delivery of the goods or, where payment of the price and delivery of the goods are to be made concurrently, if he fails to pay the price, and the seller is either in possession of the goods or otherwise able to control their disposition, the seller must take such steps as are reasonable in the circumstances to preserve them. He is entitled to retain them until he has been reimbursed his reasonable expenses by the buyer.

Article 86
(1) If the buyer has received the goods and intends to exercise any right under the contract or this Convention to reject them, he must take such steps to preserve them as are reasonable in the circumstances. He is entitled to retain them until he has been reimbursed his reasonable expenses by the seller.

(2) If goods dispatched to the buyer have been placed at his disposal at their destination and he exercises the right to reject them, he must take possession of them on behalf of the seller, provided that this can be done without payment of the price and without unreasonable inconvenience or unreasonable expense. This provision does not apply if the seller or a person authorized to take charge of the goods on his behalf is present at the destination. If the buyer takes possession of the goods under this paragraph, his rights and obligations are governed by the preceding paragraph.

Article 87
A party who is bound to take steps to preserve the goods may deposit them in a warehouse of a third person at the expense of the other party provided that the expense incurred is not unreasonable.

Article 88
(1) A party who is bound to preserve the goods in accordance with article 85 or 86 may sell them by any appropriate means if there has been an unreasonable delay by the other party in taking possession of the goods or in taking them back or in paying the price or the cost of preservation, provided that reasonable notice of the intention to sell has been given to the other party.

(2) If the goods are subject to rapid deterioration or their preservation would involve unreasonable expense, a party who is bound to preserve the goods in accordance with article 85 or 86 must take reasonable measures to sell them. To the extent possible he must give notice to the other party of his intention to sell.

(3) A party selling the goods has the right to retain out of the proceeds of sale an amount equal to the reasonable expenses of preserving the goods and of selling them. He must account to the other party for the balance.

PART IV
Final Provisions

Article 89
The Secretary-General of the United Nations is hereby designated as the depositary for this Convention.

Article 90
This Convention does not prevail over any international agreement which has already been or may be entered into and which contains provisions concerning the matters governed by this Convention, provided that the parties have their places of business in States parties to such agreement.

Article 91
(1) This Convention is open for signature at the concluding meeting of the United Nations Conference on Contracts for the International Sale of Goods and will remain open for signature by all States at the Headquarters of the United Nations, New York until 30 September 1981.
(2) This Convention is subject to ratification, acceptance or approval by the signatory States.
(3) This Convention is open for accession by all States which are not signatory States as from the date it is open for signature.
(4) Instruments of ratification, acceptance, approval and accession are to be deposited with the Secretary-General of the United Nations.

Article 92
(1) A Contracting State may declare at the time of signature, ratification, acceptance, approval or accession that it will not be bound by Part II of this Convention or that it will not be bound by Part III of this Convention.
(2) A Contracting State which makes a declaration in accordance with the preceding paragraph in respect of Part II or Part III of this Convention is not to be considered a Contracting State within paragraph (1) of article 1 of this Convention in respect of matters governed by the Part to which the declaration applies.

Article 93
(1) If a Contracting State has two or more territorial units in which, according to its constitution, different systems of law are applicable in relation to the matters dealt with in this Convention, it may, at the time of signature, ratification, acceptance, approval or accession, declare that this Convention is to extend to all its territorial units or only to one or more of them, and may amend its declaration by submitting another declaration at any time.
(2) These declarations are to be notified to the depositary and are to state expressly the territorial units to which the Convention extends.
(3) If, by virtue of a declaration under this article, this Convention extends to one or more but not all of the territorial units of a Contracting State, and if the place of business of a party is located in that State, this place of business, for the purposes of this Convention, is considered not to be in a Contracting State, unless it is in a territorial unit to which the Convention extends.
(4) If a Contracting State makes no declaration under paragraph (1) of this Article, the Convention is to extend to all territorial units of that State.

Article 94
(1) Two or more Contracting States which have the same or closely related legal rules on matters governed by this Convention may at any time declare that the Convention is not to apply to contracts of sale or to their formation where the parties have their places of business in those States. Such declarations may be made jointly or by reciprocal unilateral declarations.
(2) A Contracting State which has the same or closely related legal rules on matters

governed by this Convention as one or more non-Contracting States may at any time declare that the Convention is not to apply to contracts of sale or to their formation where the parties have their places of business in those States.
(3) If a State which is the object of a declaration under the preceding paragraph subsequently becomes a Contracting State, the declaration made will, as from the date on which the Convention enters into force in respect of the new Contracting State, have the effect of a declaration made under paragraph (1), provided that the new Contracting State joins in such declaration or makes a reciprocal unilateral declaration.

Article 95
Any State may declare at the time of the deposit of its instrument of ratification, acceptance, approval or accession that it will not be bound by subparagraph (1)(b) of article 1 of this Convention.

Article 96
A Contracting State whose legislation requires contracts of sale to be concluded in or evidenced by writing may at any time make a declaration in accordance with article 12 that any provision of article 11, article 29, or Part II of this Convention, that allows a contract of sale or its modification or termination by agreement or any offer, acceptance, or other indication of intention to be made in any form other than in writing, does not apply where any party has his place of business in that State.

Article 97
(1) Declarations made under this Convention at the time of signature are subject to confirmation upon ratification, acceptance or approval.
(2) Declarations and confirmations of declarations are to be in writing and be formally notified to the depositary.
(3) A declaration takes effect simultaneously with the entry into force of this Convention in respect of the State concerned. However, a declaration of which the depositary receives formal notification after such entry into force takes effect on the first day of the month following the expiration of six months after the date of its receipt by the depositary. Reciprocal unilateral declarations under article 94 take effect on the first day of the month following the expiration of six months after the receipt of the latest declaration by the depositary.
(4) Any State which makes a declaration under this Convention may withdraw it at any time by a formal notification in writing addressed to the depositary. Such withdrawal is to take effect on the first day of the month following the expiration of six months after the date of the receipt of the notification by the depositary.
(5) A withdrawal of a declaration made under article 94 renders inoperative, as from the date on which the withdrawal takes effect, any reciprocal declaration made by another State under that article.

Article 98
No reservations are permitted except those expressly authorized in this Convention.

Article 99
(1) This Convention enters into force, subject to the provisions of paragraph (6) of this article, on the first day of the month following the expiration of twelve months after the date of deposit of the tenth instrument of ratification, acceptance, approval or accession, including an instrument which contains a declaration made under article 92.

(2) When a State ratifies, accepts, approves or accedes to this Convention after the deposit of the tenth instrument of ratification, acceptance, approval or accession, this Convention, with the exception of the Part excluded, enters into force in respect of that State, subject to the provisions of paragraph (6) of this article, on the first day of the month following the
expiration of twelve months after the date of the deposit of its instrument of ratification, acceptance, approval or accession.
(3) A State which ratifies, accepts, approves or accedes to this Convention and is a party to either or both the Convention relating to a Uniform Law on the Formation of Contracts for the International Sale of Goods done at The Hague on 1 July 1964 (1964 Hague Formation Convention) and the Convention relating to a Uniform Law on the International Sale of Goods done at The Hague on 1 July 1964 (1964 Hague Sales Convention) shall at the same time denounce, as the case may be, either or both the 1964 Hague Sales Convention and the 1964 Hague Formation Convention by notifying the Government of the Netherlands
to that effect.
(4) A State party to the 1964 Hague Sales Convention which ratifies, accepts, approves or accedes to the present Convention and declares or has declared under article 52 that it will not be bound by Part II of this Convention shall at the time of ratification, acceptance, approval or accession denounce the 1964 Hague Sales Convention by notifying the Government of the Netherlands to that effect.
(5) A State party to the 1964 Hague Formation Convention which ratifies, accepts, approves or accedes to the present Convention and declares or has declared under article 92 that it will not be bound by Part III of this Convention shall at the time of ratification, acceptance, approval or accession denounce the 1964 Hague Formation Convention by notifying the
Government of the Netherlands to that effect.
(6) For the purpose of this article, ratifications, acceptances, approvals and accessions in respect of this Convention by States parties to the 1964 Hague Formation Convention or to the 1964 Hague Sales Convention shall not be effective until such denunciations as may be required on the part of those States in respect of the latter two Conventions have themselves become effective. The depositary of this Convention shall consult with the Government of the Netherlands, as the depositary of the 1964 Conventions, so as to ensure necessary co-ordination in this respect.

Article 100
(1) This Convention applies to the formation of a contract only when the proposal for concluding the contract is made on or after the date when the Convention enters into force in respect of the Contracting States referred to in subparagraph (1)(a) or the Contracting State referred to in subparagraph (1)(b) of article 1.
(2) This Convention applies only to contracts concluded on or after the date when the Convention enters into force in respect of the Contracting States referred to in subparagraph (1)(a) or the Contracting State referred to in subparagraph (1)(b) of article 1.

Article 101
(1) A Contracting State may denounce this Convention, or Part II or Part III of the Convention, by a formal notification in writing addressed to the depositary.
(2) The denunciation takes effect on the first day of the month following the expiration of twelve months after the notification is received by the depositary. Where a longer period for the denunciation to take effect is specified in the notification, the

denunciation takes effect upon the expiration of such longer period after the notification is received by the depositary.

Done at Vienna, this day of eleventh day of April, one thousand nine hundred and eighty, in a single original, of which the Arabic, Chinese, English, French, Russian and Spanish texts are equally authentic.

In Witness Whereof the undersigned plenipotentiaries, being duly authorized by their respective Governments, have signed this Convention.

Made in the USA
Lexington, KY
17 September 2012